Personal]
Young Adults

15 Stress-Free Tips to Craft your Financial Mindset by Budgeting, Saving Money and Investing Today

R.M. Collective

© **Copyright 2023 by R.M. Collective - All rights reserved.**

The content contained within this book may not be reproduced, duplicated or transmitted without direct written permission from the author or the publisher.

Under no circumstances will any blame or legal responsibility be held against the publisher, or author, for any damages, reparation, or monetary loss due to the information contained within this book, either directly or indirectly.

Legal Notice:

This book is copyright protected. It is only for personal use. You cannot amend, distribute, sell, use, quote or paraphrase any part, or the content within this book, without the consent of the author or publisher.

Disclaimer Notice:

Please note the information contained within this document is for educational and entertainment purposes only. All effort has been executed to present accurate, up to date, reliable, complete information. No warranties of any kind are declared or implied. Readers acknowledge that the author is not engaged in the rendering of legal, financial, medical or professional advice. The content within this book has been derived from various sources. Please consult a licensed professional before attempting any techniques outlined in this book.

By reading this document, the reader agrees that under no circumstances is the author responsible for any losses, direct or indirect, that are incurred as a result of the use of the information contained within this document, including, but not limited to, errors, omissions, or inaccuracies.

Table of Contents

FREE GUIDE:

Discover your New Mindset Today!

Managing your finances is difficult, it's even more challenging if you are doing it alone. But this time will be different. I've created an **effortless guide** to use after you finish reading each chapter. The *Personal Finance for Young Adults* guide is meant for you to stop and reflect, in hopes of empowering you to act. Download your FREE PDF by going to https://joinrmcollective.com/new-releases now!

Introduction

"Life can only be understood backwards: but it must be lived forwards," by Søren Kierkegaard.

A few years ago, I talked to a friend about how she started investing after getting her first post-college job. She had this whole mapped-out plan about how she would retire at 55, buy rental properties to create passive income, setup her 401k, and trade stocks to make it happen. I have never been more dumbfounded! She mentioned that her dad, an accountant, had taught her these skills since childhood. Then it dawned on me, being born to immigrant parents, I lacked all this knowledge.

Financial planning looks very different to people born in other parts of the world. When they immigrated, they were never given a crash course on how it works here. Immigrant parents think their kids' public school education will make up for what they don't know, but mine did not set me up for success. I was navigating the world without the proper tools to achieve my goals.

The education system in America is a beacon, luring the brightest and most aspiring young entrepreneurs from all over the world. The recipe for becoming a billionaire has become simpler over the past several decades.

Parents believe that sending their kids to college is all that's needed to achieve the American dream. That is why between 2000 and 2014, the proportion of immigrants in the U.S. with college degrees increased by 78%.

The Migrant Policy Institute, or the "think tank," found that nearly 30% of immigrants are aged 25 years and older and hold a bachelor's degree or higher (Burke, 2016).

Nevertheless, what these great universities need to do is actually teach life's essential skills of money management. Your family may even be banking on you to help them increase their finances. However, you still need to learn how to make financial planning sustainable for your family.

Even if your parents taught you all the personal finance tips and tricks you need, there is still a massive gap. Our parent generation values different things. They value stability and linear growth – work for one company for 40 years and climb the ladder. However, our generation values civic duty, fun, get it and do it now mentalities. There is a remarkable shift taking present and the future.

Establishing or building a house takes effort; much like our financial independence it needs consistent maintenance and upkeep. All of this begins with identifying what your goals are for the short and long term. Financial freedom is not a get-rich-quick-scheme; it's a life-long journey.

I have also dedicated a part of this book to women because we are often left out of the financial conversation. Don't live your life from one paycheck to the next but be open to starting your journey to enjoy the freedom and all the options life offers you right now. Take the leap, and you will never regret it!

Johann Wolfgang von Goethe once said, "Many people take no care of their money till they come nearly to the end of it, and others do just the same with their time" (BrainyQuote, 2022).

Chapter 1

Craft Your Financial Mindset

"The journey of a thousand miles begins with a single step,"
by Lao Tzu.

Building a mindset is similar to building a house. Together we will build a strong foundation that lets you kick your feet back and enjoy achieving what you've always dreamed about.

You came across this book because of a decades-old need for more understanding of personal finance. Texas A&M University conducted a research project in 2006 with four-hundred-and-seven participants. The participants took part in a basic financial evaluation where they were tested on basic financial knowledge; the average was 34.8% out of 100%.

On 9 of the 20 questions, more students were willing to accept their ignorance as they frequently chose "don't know" as an answer, with female students being in a higher percentage.

The research suggested that high school seniors need to be more equipped to handle financial matters as they currently don't understand much about personal finance (Manton et al., 2006).

Barely any educational emphasis is placed on how to manage finances, including how to start a bank account, when to take out versus to avoid loans, or how to use credit cards responsibly. If a student takes economics, accounting, or finance courses they will be exposed to financial theories. However, they will still lack practical skills.

Intention Returns to You

Oprah once said that our intentions permeate our thoughts and actions, and the intention is returned to us as a law of nature.

Additionally, we must realize that our intentions are one with the law. Oprah declared that before a specific situation or subject comes into our thoughts, it is already an intention, and it's the intention that will determine the outcome.

Oprah continued, saying, "You get to be the master of your own fate. You get to be the captain of your own soul. And if you just manage that, if you just took care of your territory.

Oh! The glorious, glorious, glorious, wondrous opportunities and possibilities that are waiting for you" (*Daily burst of energy*, 2020).

So, what's your intention with reading this book?

Are you happy to coast along and survive, or do you have dreams that aspired to fulfill? Do you have a passion in mind and a yearning to start?

Year after year, costs of living increase and debts mount, and you rarely catch up. As individuals, we need to delve into opportunities and create a financial net, to live the life we desire.

My goal is to encourage and empower you to pursue the ultimate. Nothing can't be obtained if you have a passionate desire and believe in yourself. Don't be constrained by your circumstances, work to overcome your adversities, and don't allow self-doubt and despair to creep in.

I get it; life can get overwhelming sometimes, making it feel less like we are giving up on our goals and more like we just have to survive the day. However, you need to pick your attitude and direct it to another altitude as you grow in your ability to assess and discern. Establish that strong sense of purpose, so you won't be shaken throughout your journey towards a meaningful life.

Right now, I want you to think only about yourself; are you prepared to? Don't consider anyone's expectations and especially not your closest and dearest family. Start by controlling your destiny to change the course of your life and your family's.

You may have come here because you need help paying off your credit card debt, figuring out how to take your partner on a trip to Hawaii, or how you could afford that summer music camp for your kid. Whatever it is, write it down on a post it and put it somewhere where you can see it every single day.

The following advice you are about to read in this book comes from years of research trying to help my friends, family, and even myself learn about this black hole of a topic. My goal is to get you started on your finance journey.

Throughout the book, I'll ask you to reflect on your personal and financial goals, hopefully leading to breakthroughs. You will stay motivated by frequently referring to your goals and reminding yourself why you want to achieve them because the financial road is going to take a lot of work. Don't sacrifice every single little thing to make a goal in 10 years happen that you forget to live and treat yourself. If you need a manicure occasionally to take care of yourself, do it, $50 will not break the bank, but doing it too frequently will. Below are a few more questions that you can write down and answer in this book:

- How much money do you make and spend each month?
  - Income: All money coming in
  - Expenditure: All money going out

Monthly Income	Monthly Expenditure

- What is your ideal financial situation? Please make it an achievable number.

Monthly Income	Monthly Expenditure

- How much do you want to save a month?

Current Monthly Savings	Desired Monthly Savings

It's all right to be vague when thinking about your goals since they may take a lot of work to develop initially. Besides finding ways to treat yourself throughout this process, the second secret to success is to surround yourself with positive people and a group that supports and encourages your dreams.

If you currently lack a positive community, that's also okay; it's never too late to cultivate one through social media. Before you keep reading, ensure you have everything you need to stay motivated.

Stop and finish the prompt at the end of each chapter; a couple of minutes of thinking will help ensure that you take away as much information as possible from this book.

Don't allow this book to become another one you put aside and forget about. Start by building a routine and form a new habit around your finances. Stop waiting! What's the worst that could happen?

Start the Planning Process

Designing your customized home to the exact requirements you envisioned, and have dreamt about, is one of the most fun and exhilarating projects you will undertake. Please make the most of it and revel in your creativity since, unless you are a real estate developer, you will likely only experience this process once within your lifetime.

Now is the time to start if you still need to draw up a concept. Will you make mistakes, yes, but so what? Mistakes are where you learn. The most important thing is that you start, and with action, results will follow. Theodore Roosevelt said, "The only man who never makes mistakes is the man who never does anything" (Wrightone, 2019).

Prompt

- What has stopped you in the past from getting your finances in order?

- What's the worst thing that could happen if you don't get your finances in order?

- What's the best thing that could happen if you get your finances in order?

Chapter 2
Prepare To Unlearn

"The illiterate of the 21st century will not be those who cannot read and write, but those who cannot learn, unlearn, and relearn" by Alvin Toffler.

If you are reading this book, it's because what you think you know about personal finance isn't working for you. So, keep an open mind throughout and complete all the prompts because what is the worst that could happen?

Before building a house, you must remove all the rubble stacked up on your mesmerizing waterfront land to serve as your foundation.

A "good" foundation's purpose is to give the home stability and strength that lasts more than a lifetime.

Laying a solid foundation requires more than digging a

hole or furrows and filling it with concrete. Every aspect must be flawless to ensure that the base is well-compacted and ready to lift a house up.

The way you set a house foundation is similar to how you set a new mindset. Clear all the negative doubt, old tactics that never seemed to work, and myths you've heard over the years. If you try to build a house over the layers of rocks, stones, and debris, that the environment has built up over the years; your foundation will crack.

Think of financial terminology as the material used to build your house. If you don't know what a copper pipe or cross-linked polyethylene (PEX) pipe how do you expect to know how to use them in your house? The five main terms we will use and dive deep into are income, budget, saving, spending, investing, and protection, the five main components of personal finance. These are your building materials; reference them often and make sure you know what they are and what they do.

Let's dive deeper into each one now to set your foundation.

Income

Income is an individual's source of cash flow or money coming in. It forms the foundation for the entire financial planning process. Typical sources of income, or revenue, encompass a weekly wage, hourly wages or salary, bonuses, dividends, and a pension. Income is used as the vehicle to invest, save, or spend.

Spending

Spending is money that leaves your bank account. The opposite of investments, spending is how you pay for products, services, consumables, and necessities like housing and food are your spendings. There are two ways to spend your money—cash and credit. Cash is physical, limiting you to spending only what you have. Credit is borrowed money; spend what you may or may not have and pay it back later.

The sum of money that you have access to for saving and investing is infringed on by your spending. You enter a deficit when you spend more than you earn, leaving you $0 to invest or save.

The bulk of the spending, or the lion's share, of a person's earnings, is directed to the following:

- mortgage or rent payments

- car payments

- food

- clothes

- childcare

- education

- household needs

- medical costs

- insurance

- entertainment

- travel/vacations

Saving

Savings management is a vital component of personal finances. Savings are surplus funds set aside for upcoming purchases or investments. If you spend less on your needs and have more money left over, the extra can go toward investments or savings.

First, treat and pay yourself before you save. That is a common suggestion from financial professionals because you should have the mentality that once it's in your savings account, it doesn't get touched.

It would help if you kept some savings aside to manage your financial flow and short-term disparities between income and expense. However, as savings provide little to no return compared to investments, excessive savings is not recommended.

The smartest move is to setup an automatic deposit or transaction from your paycheck to an emergency fund.

Nevertheless, remember that the recommended amount to save is up for debate and greatly depends on your situation.

Software App That Helps You to Save

Managing expenses is vital because most people have more influence over daily spending than their monthly wages.

I don't know about you, but keeping a spreadsheet and logging every single transaction I make sounds like cruel and unusual punishment. That's why I like to let technology handle that tedious task.

Mint created an app that connects to your bank accounts, logging and categorizing each transaction to help you understand where your money is going. It monitors your buying habits so that you can recognize when you start to go over budget.

Investing

Investing is the most effective technique to grow your money. Now is the time to begin conducting your study and determining whether you will start with a 401(k) or an IRA (more information in Chapter 5) retirement plan. The most essential step is to pick an account type.

Buying assets implies that over time, the investor will get back more money than they initially put in. Investments involve risk, and not all investments end up earning a profit. Typical investment types include:

- property

- private businesses

- bonds

- stocks

- mutual funds

- art

- commodities

The most complex aspect of personal finance is investing. It is also one of the most shared financial goals among young adults. Many people seek professional assistance in investing through robo-advisors or human advisors.

It's good to remember that risk and reward in various investments vary considerably.

Protection

There is a wide range of goods or products used for emergencies. When you have protection, unanticipated and unfavorable incidents are easier to navigate. Typical protective goods include:

Disability Insurance

Disability Insurance is a strategy that allows a once-off payment if you become disabled and cannot work for some time. Women qualify for this disability insurance and should claim it when they require more extended maternity leave then their work offers.

It can also work as an investment fund, focusing on a diverse range to lower the level of risk in the portfolio.

Group Risk

Group life insurance is a component of an employee benefits program. This type of insurance pays a lump sum benefit if the policyholder is identified as having one of the specific illnesses on a predetermined list.

Insurance that benefits policyholders who are unable to work due to illness or accident is known as income protector insurance. A life insurance policy is a legal agreement between the insured and the insurer. The other two protections I want to mention are:

- health insurance

- estate preparation

When a variety of protection is actively maintained, it stops sector-specific events from impacting the overall portfolio.

This aspect of personal finance frequently necessitates expert guidance, as navigating and making the most informed decisions can be tricky. For instance, a wide range of analyses must be conducted to analyze a person's estate planning and insurance needs. Speak to your company's Human Resources team to learn more about your benefits and how to set your protections up correctly for your circumstances.

The Practice of Personal Financial Planning

The key to sound money management is having a strategy and following it. A budget or a formal financial plan will include all the aspects mentioned above. In general, the following listed below are the main phases in the process of financial planning:

- Assess

- Plan

- Set

- Implement

- Monitor and Review

Your best chance of attaining personal and family goals will depend on you creating a budget or financial plan.

Financial Freedom

We recognize that gaining financial freedom means paying off all our debts. Zero debt will help us accumulate a security net when saving and generating enough passive income from investing or operating a business to cover current and anticipated future living costs.

We are consistently distracted from achieving our most important financial goals by mounting debt, financial emergencies, spending, and unexpected bills payments. Universally, we all face these difficulties, but by adopting the behaviors to prepare for life's surprises, you can be on the path to financial wellness.

Debt is like having poor weather throughout your house-building process. It will take you longer for the concrete to dry if it's constantly pouring; and it will continue to cost you more time and energy when you must keep fixing things that fall apart before you put the roof up.

Create a plan to insert inroads to achieve your life's goals, both big and small, financial and as lifestyle related. Plan your finances so you have enough money to care for all your necessities and desires. Follow through with the next strategy, pay off your credit cards in full and leave yourself with as little debt as possible, then start to monitor your expenses.

Live within your means.

Data from a 2019 study about family wealth defined specific attributes determining if a family knew less about Consumer Finances. We based a family's demographics on the attributes of the study participants, who are typically the members of a household that are the most literate in personal finances.

All racial and ethnic groups were considered in the study, and higher education was linked to a higher income. There are still significant discrepancies at every educational level, with Black and Hispanic families generally having lower median accumulated wealth than white families with a comparable education degree.

Compared to white families, Black and Hispanic families are far less inclined to own a wide variety of assets (such as more than one vehicle, businesses, homes, and financial and retirement assets). If they did, those assets are more likely to be of less value.

Evidence demonstrates that systemic impediments and discriminatory behaviors are unlikely to be considerably reduced by individual actions or minor policy changes. In decreasing inequalities and in boosting "Black and Hispanic" income, more remarkable systemic adjustments (PDF) are required (Hernandez- Kent & R. Ricketts, 2021).

Andrew Tudor, CFP, creator of Alchemist Wealth, focuses on assisting Black families in bridging the racial wealth gap. Andrew stated that most of his white clients begin with wealthy family members who contributed their finances to investments in their 20s and 30s.

According to data from EducationData.org for 2021, Black college graduates default on their loans at higher rates than white students. They also owe an average of $25,000 more in student loan debt.

Historically, white people may utilize their earnings to start investing right away. In contrast, many Black people start with a negative amount (Foster, 2022). This book aims to equip you with the resources to develop a positive financial mindset for your household and yourself, regardless of age, race, or gender. Managing your set of financial beliefs is involved in the income group below.

Abundant Resources or Assets

Investments in stocks, valuable property, and cash kept in the bank are assets that enable financial freedom. You first need to invest in assets, typically vast sums of money over a lengthy period, before using them to achieve financial freedom.

For instance, most financial advisors say that your contributions to a pension fund are directed explicitly at long-term security and stability. If individuals start investing early, many will find this to be a significant benefit in the long run.

Those who waited until their 50th birthday or later to begin investing will benefit less from the years of compounded interest. Usually, their contributions will stay the same or only slightly increase.

Another issue is that if you spend all your assets too quickly, you won't have enough left to pay your expenses. In addition to accumulating sufficient assets in the stock market and the housing market, you will likely receive an extra source of income from areas such as social security, dividend-paying, a business, or securities that you invested in. These will give you additional financial security.

Here are a few terms that will help you in understanding investing:

- **Stocks:** fractional interests that are bought in a corporation

- **Equities:** stocks or ownership interests in a business

  o Purchasing stocks entails purchasing equity. When you become an employee of a new company, you could also receive "equity."

- **Bonds:** are typically considered less risky than stocks

  o However, the risk associated with stocks can vary significantly from one firm to another corporation. Bonds function similarly to corporate IOUs.

- **Real Estate:** Purchasing property to rent out is another form of investing.

- **Businesses:** refers to a prolonged activity carried out to generate income.

  o It can also refer to managing finances and affairs or business activities.

- **Cash:** the conditions of a business deal that uses available money.

- **Budget:** A budget or financial plan can serve as an overview of managing your finances. Making and sticking to a monthly household budget proposal ensures that all expenses are paid and that investments and the development of independent income are progressing as planned.

- **Pay Your Obligations and Debts:** This includes your student loans, mortgage, car loan, and comparable loans that typically increase over time with interest.

  o These mentioned loans are substantially lower than those of credit cards, rendering a less risky situation in your finances. The exact opposite of freedom is being buried under debt for years. After all, debt implies duty and even servitude, both opposing the concept of financial freedom.

- **Mindset Adjustment:** This is the term used to adopt a culture of saving by using a significant mindset.

  o Most people are unwilling to adjust and alter their ways and others don't comprehend the problem. It doesn't get any simpler or easier to save as you age, so now is the time to act. Over time, your salary might have doubled, but your assets need to keep up with your new earnings. The more you make, the more you should invest and grow your assets.

- **Life Goals:** These are realistic dreams you have for

your life.

- o Write down the amount of money needed to create the lifestyle or standard of living that you are used to. Include the year you hope to reach your goal, and how long you anticipate raising the necessary funds. Your prospects of achieving goals will increase with how specific they are. Then, move back to your current age and set regular financial checkpoints. These could include specific sums of money saved or assets that are accumulated. If this didn't make sense to you, remember that's why apps like Betterment exist; they do the math for you. All you have to do is download and set it up.

Stay up to Date on Trends

Stay current on news and developments in the world of finance, and don't be afraid to make necessary adjustments to your investment portfolio.

The most vital safeguard against people who prey on ignorant consumers is knowledge.

Ensure you know your credit limit while using your credit card to prevent overspending. Additionally, learn to be aware of the following:

- **Look after your possessions:** Everything from cars to lawnmowers to shoes and clothing needs to be cared for. All your belongings will survive longer when you take proper care of them. Taking care of them means getting your oil changed regularly, sewing the barely noticeable hole in your shirt, and not slamming the brakes every time you drive.

  o Your home and assets need to be maintained on a regular basis. Imagine not having to purchase clothing and shoes as frequently as you do. Regular upkeep will help you save money because you won't need to replace them as often.

- **Live within your means:** You should only spend a certain amount allocated in your budget that comes from your income. It's easier than it may appear to live frugally by adopting the mentality of getting the most out of life with the least amount of resources. Many affluent people live modestly compared to how much they earn. That is often one reason why many people are wealthy today.

  o Frugality does not preclude adopting a spartan lifestyle or calling for excessive hoarding or garbage diving. Frugality is the prudent acquisition of only buying what you absolutely need.

- **Take care of your holistic well-being:** This intends to make you aware that health cannot be acquired; you only get one body to use in this life. When health and well-being become a standard component of your life, you become more efficient, engaged, and productive and less likely to miss work or get injured on the job.

  - ○ Your income could suffer when you run out of sick days at work. Ailments and health issues drive up insurance costs, and poor health may necessitate an early retirement with reduced monthly payments.

  - ○ Being healthy means you could select a lower health insurance premium, you are physically able to complete house tasks and don't need to hire help, and you likely won't have unexpected trips to the urgent care.

You'll never finish building your house if you are busy at the doctor's office.

———

Three Tips to Building Your New Financial Mindset

Tip 1: Learn How and When to Say No!

It can be incredibly difficult to say no, especially if you identify as a people-pleaser. You can be asked to do a favor for a friend or to stand in for a co-worker as they need help with shifts.

How do you respectfully assert yourself without feeling bad—or worse, feel forced into doing something that puts you and your family's plan at risk?

Many people take chances and put unnecessary demands on others, and often targeting those who battle to say "no." When you decline their request, you are not being rude. After all, the task is their responsibility, and the onus is on them to complete it. You must respect your feelings and life, not just for yourself but for your loved ones.

Be assertive and take control of your emotions. Create a margin in that space between yourself and your limits. It's not a privilege to have your own life; it's a right!

Try using this template: "Thank you so much for considering me to do {insert their ask}, however, I respectfully have to decline as I have to prioritize {insert 1-3 things that hold greater weight for you}."

Tip 2: Prepare for the Unexpected

The capacity to save and put money aside for a rainy day or unexpected events is essential, as we can't control the future. Look at COVID-19, for instance, which caused historically high unemployment rates that reached 4.9% in October 2021. We couldn't have predicted its aftermath.

A Pulse survey found that in October 2021, 12 million adults who rented houses or apartments were in arrears – owed money - on their rent. Close to 20 million adults that resided in families didn't have sufficient food to eat.

Some economic progressions extended to late March as other financial provisions stagnated. The economy became further influenced as unemployment benefit payments lapsed and expired. High costs were incurred on numerous items in supply grocery store chains (Center on budget and policy priorities, 2021).

Tip 3: Take Accountability for your Life and Decisions

Have the confidence to declare, "I am totally and solely accountable for my financial choices." Our parents, teachers, and experiences may or may not have taught us about financial planning. However, as adults, we can no longer cast the blame and hold them accountable. We need to find the answers and start correcting the past.

Let Go of These Myths

The old saying that the rich stay rich while the poor stay poor is a fallacy. It is possible to learn about finances, and you can become wealthy if you're willing to learn, have hard conversations, and make changes to your lifestyle. However, we tend to adopt our parents' and our friends' financial habits and mindsets. Check out the list of myths below:

- The more money you make, the better off you are.

- You are too young for bad things to happen.

- Short-term satisfaction is always worth it.

We also need to change our mindset that bad things can't happen because we are young. It's often noticeable among the youth; they believe they are immortal and aren't serious about unforeseen situations or their money matters. They can have fun all month long, and don't need to concern themselves with any real responsibility.

Unfortunately, that is not how the world works. No one is promised a carefree life and unfortunately bad things do happen to good and young people. As young adults, we often feel the need to satisfy our impulses, but treating yourself every day will impact you long-term.

Is short-term satisfaction worth it? Evidence indicates that short-term satisfaction is quickly forgotten, just like you already forgot the feeling of getting your nails done as you pick your cuticles. However, long-term satisfaction provides you comfort for decades. We may initially feel fantastic after receiving a distinguished award, a sizable raise, a promising new relationship, a luxurious new car, or losing weight. However, the height of happiness doesn't stay or last long (Smith, 2020).

Humans are eager to change with the times, which has enabled us to survive and flourish. However, it also implies that the good things that first make us happier quickly become our new norm, and we revert to our previous level of happiness.

Experts in positive psychology have discovered that you can increase your level of happiness and life satisfaction. Have you heard of how most lottery winners end up depressed and broke; it's because they staked their happiness on one winning, but it was short lived. Happiness requires an inward shift in perception and attitude. And the reality is that anyone can do it.

Another myth I want to discuss relates to having more money, as money is meant to bring happiness, but did you know that time is what truly does? Let me ask you, how often have you voluntarily given up your free time to stay late at work? Did missing time with your pet, kids, or partner make you happy? According to recent studies, valuing cash over time makes us less happy, and more money often equals more problems.

In the latest study, over 1,000 graduating British Columbia students took part in a test to determine whether people value their dollars more than their free time. Most students said they prioritized time, but nearly 40% said they put money first (Dunn & Courtney, 2020).

The students were asked, when considering everything, how content they were. The student's level of satisfaction was assessed twice, once before they graduated and again later, to determine how this decision connected to their cognitive and emotional health.

In addition to other measurements, individuals were asked a few questions and told to consider everything. Finally, they were asked how satisfied they were with life in general.

The outcome ranged from 0 to 10, where 0 represents not at all, and 10 represents extreme content. Researchers discovered that students who prioritized money were less content within a year of graduation than their peers who emphasized time (Dunn & Courtney, 2020).

After considering their diverse socioeconomic origins and adjusting their level of contentment prior to graduation, the results held true. Naturally, you should accept the next raise you get, but you should also not work 24/7 to get it.

A ton of data supports the idea that happier individuals are more prosperous, but having a greater income will not always make you happier. Your level of happiness with money is influenced by how you use, manage, and think about it. Below is Elon Musk's life story; he claims that he has found happiness regardless of the money.

Elon Musk's Story

Elon Musk, born in Pretoria, South Africa, in 1971, took the world by storm.

He was an astonishing teenager who was always busy with his computer. At the age of 12, che reated a video game and sold it to a computer magazine.

In 1988, he obtained a Canadian passport knowing it would be easier for him to come to the United States this way. He believed that the U.S. economy had more opportunities to offer him. In 1995, he founded the Zip2 company while he was still busy studying. Zip2 provided maps and business directories to online newspapers (Mint, 2023).

He received his bachelor's degree in physics and economics in 1997. In 1999, Elon and his brother sold Zip2 for an impressive $307 million. He lost no time and went on to found another online financial services company called X.com, which later became PayPal. An online auction sold this company and upped Elon's bank account by a staggering $1.5 billion in 2002.

Musk is convinced that humanity needs multiple planets to survive on. He is now busying himself in several businesses to achieve this. His focus is on making space rockets more affordable.

He has also manufactured a hyperloop pod but isn't diverting his interest from SpaceX and Tesla to continue with its manufacture. Here are a few "multibillion" suggestions from Musk:

- Musk's recommendation on Twitter stated, "never affix yourself to anyone or any place, business, or project. Only commit yourself to a mission, one calling, one purpose. That is how you maintain your authority and peace" (Mint, 2023).

- Tosca Musk the founder, and CEO of the streaming service Passionflix has frequently thanked her brother for his "precious" counsel. Tosca claimed that Elon once advised her that she should pay close attention to those who are investing in her firm since, in a way, she will be married to them forever.

- Elon Musk advises young people never to choose a job based on the likelihood that it will make them famous. Instead, he advised them to concentrate on something more straightforward: locate a career that suits your abilities and something you enjoy, and are good at.

- Avoid attempting to lead simply for the sake of leading. Often, individuals want a leadership position, but don't actually want to be in those positions once they learn what they entail. The Tesla CEO claims that a desire to be in the spotlight won't always be beneficial.

Elon Musk is one of the wealthiest men in the world, but it all started with how he chose to be creative in his time.

Prompt

- What is the one thing you currently find most challenging with your finances? Is it budgeting? Is it saving? Is it something else? If you attempt to tackle every aspect of your personal finance off the bat, you will fail. Start with one—get that ball rolling smoothly and move on to the next.

- Why has that one thing been so difficult for you to deal with?

Chapter 3
Lay The Foundation

"You are never too old to start over. Every day is a chance to make changes to create the life we want," by Karon Waddell.

Let's start building your personal finances.

It is often easier to believe that things will magically fall into place. One morning, you will wake up and now can afford to buy a house or retire early—that's wishful thinking.

Perhaps by reading this book, your goal is to start taking your more seriously or want some guidance on where to start.

A handful of people are truly aware of what a poverty mindset is, and several communities still believe that they can't change their financial status. We see the repercussions, such as unemployment, overcrowding, and all society's evils, yet we frequently miss the worst parts. Some of us get away without experiencing those repercussions and think we are fine, so we don't prepare.

Most of the time, those with a poor mindset accomplish nothing because they believe they have nothing to offer. These people wait for a way out or someone to help them. Generations are stuck in this cycle and barely manage to keep themselves alive. However, don't you see, it's just their mindset. They would be open to more opportunities if they started thinking they could change their circumstances. And so can you!

Look at Bomikazi Madikizela's story demonstrating how a nonconventional thinking style can influence future generations in an underdeveloped rural area.

Bomikazi is 29 years old and grew up in South Africa in the village of Bizana, a rural area of what used to be the Transkei region. Her grandmother raised her so her mother could remain in school. Bomikazi claimed that her grandmother played the most significant role in changing her life.

She was taught to work the land and use what they had with their hands and mind. She began farming at the tender age of six, and they only ate the food from their garden.

They grew amadumbe (a starch root), mealies, beans, and

veggies. The produce was occasionally sold to pay for other foods, or the cash was used to buy farming supplies. Bomikazi said the amadumbe crop was quite successful! Her mother was the only child to get a degree among her five siblings. So, her mother motivated her to work hard at school so she, too, could be awarded a scholarship to continue her education.

Bomikazi was not only able to finish her schooling with a National Diploma (a high-grade percentage certificate that allows entry to a university in South Africa), but she received a scholarship to study analytical chemistry in 2013. In 2015, she graduated from Nelson Mandela University with a B Tech degree in chemistry.

After graduating, Bomikazi was offered employment at Aspen Pharmacare in Port Elizabeth (P.E South Africa) the same year she joined as a Junior Laboratory Analyst. By 2018, she was promoted to Senior Laboratory Analyst.

She learned about WORK 4 A LIVING (W4AL) that same year. Then, she bought a two-bedroom apartment since she didn't want to rent.

When Bomikazi first heard about WORK 4 A LIVING, one of her friends was staying with her. Her friend decided to take a W4AL course while job hunting. In the evenings, Bomikazi's friend would often come back to the apartment from her course so invigorated.

This energy sparked Bomikazi's interest, and she wanted to know more as she planned to open a training facility in her hometown of Bizana. Ena, from the W4AL course, suggested that Bomikazi first enroll to observe the facilitation style.

She already lived a hectic life, but with her passion to change her life, she made plans to work night shifts to take the course and assist her friends back home who were struggling with their English.

Bomikazi claims that W4AL helped her recognize that they have everything they need to enhance their lives and that there is no reason for people to continue living in poverty.

Bomikazi said that many of the young people within her nation have this attitude of entitlement; They believe that the government, the educational system, or their parents should take action to improve their lives.

She went on to say that she discovered that once a person begins to think nobody owes them anything, their mind alters, and they become liberated.

In addition to working full-time and mentoring for W4AL, she is pursuing a Postgraduate Certificate in Education (PGCE) with an emphasis on physical sciences and mathematics. She intends to complete her education within the year before returning to Bizana.

In addition to opening a W4AL training facility, she aims to impart her farming and computer skills to the next generation. Bomikazi claims that her people believe they are underprivileged and unfit to perform tasks such as math and science, as they claim the subjects are too complicated. Hence, they already decided to quit before giving themselves a chance.

She aims to impart to children and young adults the knowledge she has received from her grandmother. She wants to inspire others, just like her mother and grandmother did for her. Bomikazi believes that through her faith, she has everything she requires to help communities prosper economically, educationally, and agriculturally (Davel, 2020).

Are You Struggling?

Are you struggling to break the parental or social mindset around how you should spend your money? You may have heard your parents say, "Live every day as though it's your last." Accumulate these memories as that's what you are left with at the end, but you still need a plan and balance to achieve your current and future goals.

You see, when building a structure, it should withstand various forces that act on it. These forces include shear torsion, tension, compression, and bending.

Load combinations, earthquake load, and deadweight

must all be considered. The technique of framing entails joining construction components to produce a strong structure.

These components include studs, rafters, plates, joists, headers, girders, and flooring, which act interchangeably. All these factors are balanced and work towards building a solid house.

On the other side of the spectrum, regarding your finances, you might have strict parents who believe you should save everything. They might have rolled their eyes when you wanted something to buy a new dress or wanted to go to a fancy dinner with friends.

This imbalance could be another reason you act conservatively. You are afraid to take risks in your investment. Certain people from modest backgrounds find it challenging to take any form of risk as it makes them nervous.

I don't know your background, only you do, and by understanding yourself, you will find healing, adapt, and progress. Money success has nothing to do with intelligence, education, or math prowess.

It has to do with trying; certain people are more likely to exhibit these habits than others. When you become conscious of your patterns, you can use the strength of your mind, and your thoughts will transform your life in tangible ways.

Break these family cycles and stop saying, "Well my parents had nothing, but they had each other." We are more likely to motivate ourselves to grow and accomplish our financial goals if we know the strengths, perspectives, limitations, and inclinations we bring to the table.

Your money is handled in the same way. Go and build generational wealth to leave a legacy for your future children and grandchildren; look for a refresher on your finances and reset it. Either way, it's better to take a frame down made of particle board than to watch your house collapse. Don't build the entire house just to discover that you installed a pipe wrong and now have major water damage.

Let's start at the very beginning and build your house's foundation to last. Below, we will start to talk about the first three components of personal finance. This book won't delve into the protection aspect, which includes health and life insurance, as they are quite advanced.

Some states often require health insurance for tax purposes, so please google your state and check or seek professional advice regarding protection. This is not a risk you want to take.

Generate an Income

When you generate an income, you engage in work that will bring in money. You will be doing this for most of your life, so find enjoyable and meaningful work if you can. The reason is that you will perform better and be eager to get to work in the mornings. Your career will develop quicker, and you will continue to do the work for a more extended period. All these factors will increase your chances of financial success.

In fact, research revealed that more than 90% of workers stated they would return a portion of their earning potential for a job position with more job satisfaction and personal enjoyment (World commission on environment and development, 1987).

Once a year, at the very least, analyze if your present salary covers all the expenses and if you still have money left to save. As soon as you land a new job, you should assess your financial situation, fulfillment, and enjoyment. Ask yourself these questions below:

- Will my salary grow at a realistic rate if I remain with my current employer?

- Can I do better in the field I am in?

- Can I work towards a higher level, or are other options

available?

- Does this work bring me joy?

If you are starting to question your current career, ask yourself if your situation can change without finding a new job. Can a conversation with your boss alleviate the problem, and will it put you back on track for a higher income, or is this a role with no growth opportunities?

If it is, start researching and applying. Don't be spontaneous in your actions; act responsibly, and make sure you have another opportunity lined up before taking any drastic action.

Saving and Spending

You know yourself well enough to know if your tendency is to spend or save a lot. Overspending may be a coping strategy for deeper-rooted trauma. Think about the root cause of your habits and seek professional help to find healthier ways to manage them.

If you feel like your money is will burn a hole in your wallet if you don't use it, you start to dream about how wonderful that new leather coat or couch will be in your possession. This is when you know that something needs to change.

On the contrary, a saver's first impulse is to refrain from making purchases. They are considerably happy now that they have money saved, and savers can wait patiently before making a purchase.

If you prioritize saving, ensure that you do it with a balance in mind. Don't save everything and sacrifice moments of enjoyment. With a balanced mentality, you can achieve long-term satisfaction.

You might have witnessed or overheard your parents speak about finances or have gone through a tough time with your finances—or no one has mentioned money at all. Although it won't entirely describe your financial thinking, it's still important to be aware of the situation.

As an illustration of how a prior experience can result in adult money disputes: Does it irritate you and cause arguments when your partner spends money on things you don't think is unnecessary? It might be as simple as a particular brand of toilet paper or an expensive handbag.

Going overboard can be risky for both spenders and savers. If you are a spender and spend everything you earn, you will go bankrupt. And savers, if you hold onto every penny you earn, you might miss out on various enjoyable activities that make your life happy and meaningful.

When we consider it, the situation seems clear; however, the issue is that we still need to consider finding a solution and a healthy balance.

Many of us are conditioned from a young age, in school or higher education establishments, to do things a certain way.

The word "budget" could cause a positive reaction to some, but to others, it can cause a perplexed reaction.

If you are the free spirit type, the category under shopping and amusement is your love language. People with a free spirit prefer to live wildly and without constraint!

The conservative type will hold onto their finances as security. As you can see, both sides can learn from each other. Find someone who thinks differently than you regarding finances and have a conversation about their motivations. You never know what you'll find.

Is your status motivating or driving you? You might need to have a serious heart-to-heart on this issue. Be sincere with yourself whenever you consider what drives you to spend or save. Allow the psychology of finances to work for you and find out how money motivates you.

When we investigate the safety-conscious or saver's way of thinking, money is desired for security. This mentality is formulated out of fear; it may be the fear of employment, a severe illness, or a decreased income. Beware of living in fear if you are a "safe spender."

Fear can prevent you from making charitable contributions when you have the money. Donations are tax-deductible; you are likely losing out on money each year for not being charitable. It can also stop you from saving money for your retirement or purchasing a new pair of shoes once the old ones start to fall apart.

Money has a way of enhancing one's sense of self. Being courteous and giving will make you more liberal with cash. You will act far more arrogant and self-conscious with money if you already possess signs of those characteristics. You have the freedom to choose how you want to use money; Money is just a tool.

The psychology of money impacts hundreds of small decisions we make every day without you even recognizing it. The safety vs. status trend is one instance that comes to mind.

Some will gravitate toward status and will only be interested in a product if in some way, their purchase creates a sense of success. An example is when you say, "I want a Lexus because everyone I know has a Lexus."

These people will often figure out ways to rationalize a more expensive purchase. This may merely indicate that they enjoy fine things and believe me, having lovely things is perfectly fine if you can afford them.

However, it would be best if your kept your expenditures in check since this can lead to a predisposition toward status. Keep in mind that who you are is not defined by the things you have.

Three Tips to Managing Your Income

You will better understand how and where you spend your money once you actively manage your finances. This will enable you to stick to your spending plan and grow your savings when placing your finances into a percentage-based system.

Learning to manage your money well will help you to reach your financial goals by practicing good personal finance management and success.

Tip 1: Understand What You Need Financially to Achieve Your Goals

- Do you need to save $10,000 to buy a new car?

- Do you need to save $50,000 for a down payment on a house?

- Do you need to be able to put aside $500 a month to

pay off your debt?

When you are not sure what you need, stop and do some research. Once you have an idea, come back to the drawing board. Having a goal drives you to stay motivated. Pick a realistic date or framework to achieve a set amount needed to achieve your goal and write it down, so you remember.

Tip 2: Pick a Realistic Framework

Here are four frameworks that you can use to get started. Keep in mind that you can switch between them to reach short-term vs. long-term goals.

1. *The 50/30/20 framework:*

- Background: The 50/30/20 budgeting rule was made popular by U.S. Senator Elizabeth Warren in her book, *All Your Worth: The Ultimate Lifetime Money Plan.* According to the guideline, 50% of your after-tax income should be used on needs, 30% towards wants, and 20% on savings (Whiteside, 2022).

    o This simple and logical approach will assist you in creating a realistic budget that you can follow over time to reach your financial goals.

- The 50% categorizes the absolute "must haves." These include mortgage or rent payments, food expenses, auto loans, insurance, medical expenses, minimal debt payments, and utility bills.

- The remaining 50% should be divided into 30% for anything else you choose; this includes eating out or getting takeout, Netflix, cable, going to the movies, that pearl bracelet, Christmas gifts, sports equipment or events, partying, or taking a vacation.

- The last 20% must be divided into two, 10% must go toward savings, and the last 10% for debt reduction or savings if you don't have any debt.

It's best to pay off high-interest debt before spending 30% on entertainment or 10% on investments. Few investments will yield returns as high as credit card fees, so start with that first.

2. *The 70/20/10 framework:*

This framework divides your income into three key percentage areas. The most significant portion, 70%, is allocated to living expenditures. The next 20% is used for debt repayment or savings, and 10% goes to debt repayment, donations, or fun.

- The majority, 70%, goes toward daily expenses; including mortgage or rent payments, food expenses, auto loans, insurance, medical expenses, minimal debt payments, and utility bills.

- The 20% goes toward investments or savings.

- The last 10% goes towards debt repayment or donations. Once the debt is cleared, the funds can go towards a fun bucket or savings.

The 70/20/10 guideline can be complemented by employing another budget strategy called bucketing. This method helps you care for your essential requirements, debt, and financial goals.

Bucketing is when you divide your income by the percentages into their specific accounts. With bucketing, you are likely to manage your everyday expenses better as you will stay in control of your debt and have the potential to save by splitting your money into these predetermined categories.

Try to put as much into debt, striving to pay off the entire sum. This rule helps people manage their finances and set aside funds for a pension and other unexpected expenses.

By the third quarter of 2020, Americans owed a staggering $14.9 trillion in debt -something to think about (Fay, 2021).

3. Zero-Based Budget:

Start by assigning every dollar into a category so there is never a surplus. Categories can be as specific as rent and eating out or as broad as necessities, wants, and savings. It's a strategy utilized by businesses, but it has been adopted successfully by private individuals and families.

Set a specific time every month to work on your financial situation and work out what your requirements are. Usually, people keep this till the end of a month to reflect on their previous month's spending and plan for the upcoming month.

4. *Value-Based Budget:*

This entails creating a detailed financial plan that is based on your priorities.

- Look at this scenario below and think about what this person values.

  o Living expenses: 52%

  o Debt: 10%

  o Eating out: 15%

  o Shopping: 17%

  o Travel: 6%

- Now, write down your values. Are they accurately represented in your budget?

- For example, here are three things I value and prioritize in my budget:

- Giving back to my community

- Investing in real estate

- Traveling

Tip 3: Commit

Choose a system that will work for you. Set the clock and work it out. Commit to this way of budgeting for at least 6 months to see change! Keep in mind that these frameworks don't have to be "forever situations," so change them based on what your situation and goals amount to. Here are a few examples of how 2 people I know used these frameworks:

1. Yasmine wanted to buy a home in Detroit. She is 25 years old, single, and making $60k annually. She follows the rule of 3—buy a home up to 3X her gross salary to afford a $180k home. Yasmine wants to save $36k for a down payment and $10k for closing costs. There is an additional $10k set aside in case anything goes wrong.

   o **Her Goal:** Save $56k in 4 years.

   o **Framework:** Zero-Based Budget—this prompts her to be aggressive in her saving, and she decides to set aside 35% of her income annually. She was motivated by the goal, so it was easy to say no to short-term gratifications like going out every Friday with friends.

2. Jonas wants to save up to take his wife and son from Texas to North Carolina to visit his family for Christmas. He is 27 years old, married, has 1 child, and making $80k annually.

   o **His Goal:** Save $3k in 3 months. However, since his son is a 1-year-old and his expenses fluctuate, Jonas needs a flexible budget. He also has $25k in student loans that he needs to pay towards each month.

   o **Framework**: 70/20/10

Jonas needs to save $1k within a month which is 20% of his net pay; therefore, this framework will work for him. While his budget methods can be switched based on his goals, savings should be a constant part of his finance management.

You can change your budgeting strategies depending on your goals; however, saving must always be a part of your routine money management. Even if you don't have anything you are saving for now, that is okay; save anyway, because emergencies do come up and you never know what next month has planned for you.

———

Three Tips to Saving

1. Set your savings amount to autopay into a separate bank account each month, so that you never have to think about it. Make sure it's a high-yield savings account like Ally.

2. Don't expand your lifestyle if your income changes; put that straight into savings.

3. Search for different utility and insurance companies; you won't believe the discounts you will find.

Richard Branson's Story

Billion-dollar advice from the founder of Virgin, Richard Branson.

Most people love him and are so inspired by him. His unassuming manner makes him a world-class leader who expects quality, but never has a bad word to say.

Growing up, Branson had severe dyslexia, and it caused poor academic achievement. He left school at 16 and on the last day, Robert Drayson, his school's headmaster, said, "Richard you will either go to jail or you will be a millionaire."

At 15, even though Richard was challenged in reading and writing, he never let it deter him from starting his own publication for youngsters his age. He wanted to know what was happening in the business world, and desired the chance to influence change. He said, "I felt that I could get out and start creating things that would make a difference in the world" (Wiener-Bronner, 2018).

So, the young Richard Branson started mailing records to customers for a price to fund his publications. The publication eventually failed; however, Virgin Records took hold and was established in 1979, out of the mail-order music industry.

Richard said, "I went to 7 record companies, and none of them would put this [Tubular Bells] out. So, I formed a little record company on my own" (Wiener-Bronner, 2018). Following the release of *Tubular Bells*, the risks paid off. Richard recalled, "It sold millions and millions of albums."

He went on to sign-up unknowns that no one else wanted, and they became popular acts like the *Sex Pistols*, *The Rolling Stones*, and *Janet Jackson*. After 10 years of making Virgin Records a great success, Richard changed course.

Why not fly high, he thought. So, Richard bought into the airlines. He claimed that nobody believed the company would survive after he opened Virgin Airs. Howver, Virgin proved good enough to attract clients.

The overall market in airline services performed terribly at the time, and Virgin Airs developed a service that people cherished. He claimed that people made special efforts to go on Virgin America. Then, once Virgin Australia opened its doors, which is part of the global Virgin travel family, the same thing happened, and it has grown over time.

He is currently working alongside Virgin Unite as well as all the other organizations it has launched. These organizations include *The B team, Elders, Ocean Unite*, and other enterprises that will have a positive impact on the world, such as space travel. Richard is aiming for commercial space flight via Virgin Galactic.

He is reluctant to lag a great deal behind SpaceX CEO Elon Musk, an adversary in the space industry. Richard claims this is regarding a Tesla roadster that Musk launched into space in conjunction with SpaceX's Falcon Heavy rocket's inaugural flight.

Richard has had quite a few pitfalls when growing his wealth; Virgin Group first made Virgin Cola available to the general population in 1994. In a 2014 blog article, Richard declared that a fizzy drink battle against Coke was insane. He admitted that the cola business became one of his biggest failures.

Richard also concluded that his biggest fault was that Virgin Cola was not distinctive enough from the big-time Coke product. Virgin now only joins a market once it believes it can begin offering something vastly different, which will ultimately up-end the market.

However, Richard doesn't view failure negatively, states that failure is a fantastic learning method to become an entrepreneur. He also said, "You simply can't accomplish anything if you don't take chances" (Wiener-Bronner, 2018). So, what if occasionally he has had to learn it a different way?

He would instead attempt something than do nothing at all. "If you give something a go and it doesn't work out, you certainly haven't failed," he said. "You just learned" (Wiener-Bronner, 2018). Richard has left some good advice for us below to follow.

Try one of those frameworks a try, and who knows what you will learn along the way.

Prompt

- What is one goal you are determined to achieve this year:

- Write down the dollar amount that is tied to e goal above.

- What is one excuse that might prevent you from attaining your goal? Write it on a sheet of paper, then tear it up and get it out of your head.

- Decide on which method to create your monthly budget – an app, spreadsheet, or pen and paper.

Stop here before reading on and go set it up! Right now!

Chapter 4
Make It Functional

"Hoping for the best, prepared for the worst, and unsurprised by anything in between" by Maya Angelou.

Unforeseen circumstances are part of life. Nobody plans for their windshield to be hit by a rock and crack, their child to get sick, or their pipes to freeze. But, these things happen, and it's on you to be prepared for any of them, or else you'll end up with serious debt and stress. This is where an emergency fund can assist you in covering unexpected costs that go beyond your regular living expense.

Knowing that you can cover a few additional expenses will put your mind at ease. Moreover, you can pay for expenditures without using your credit card or obtaining a personal loan. Below is a story about how Margaret Sutton overcame her difficult times.

This was Margaret Sutton's account of events when she was terminated. "On March 31, between 3:30 pm and 4 pm, one lazy afternoon at the pool while visiting my girlfriend, I received a call. The president and owner of my firm called. He told me that my job would be terminated immediately.

He said that, due to the economic slump, the company is going to have to do without my position. The work I did will be absorbed by the other staff members. The small, family-run company that I worked for had to undergo significant changes due to the Covid aftermath.

After working at the firm for 30 years and being in leadership for almost 20 years, I thought I would be safe. Wasn't I part of the future? I was the Senior Vice President of Client Services.

COVID-19 significantly impacted my position because the bulk of the clients I worked with were employed in the airline industry. Just like that, it was all gone!

It still came as a terrible shock, and I felt rejected when I was hit with news from someone I was inspired to be. The people I collaborated and worked with were like my family, and they will be greatly missed. Also, I've never been unemployed the entire time during my working career. I didn't know where to start.

Fortunately, I opened an emergency account, and paid a year's worth of my salary into it. Over the years, it gained interest. I considered closing it at one stage, but boy am I glad I didn't! The money has been a lifesaver and an absolute comfort to my family and I.

I asked for my retirement fund to be transferred so that I could keep paying into it. At my age, I will be relying on it in the next twelve years, so I couldn't afford to not invest. The worst was having to tell my kids about my termination, as it was a first for me.

My girls were studying, so they were dependent on me for everything. We found that maintaining optimism and going forward was the most important thing, as it made our minds clear to receive solutions.

My family and I are content and secure because we work closely with a budget. I even started consulting for companies, and month over month I receive more and more work.

My family has changed a few things. For instance, we were not incredibly frivolous when purchasing food, whereas now we are careful. We have been visiting thrift shops and are open to purchasing second-hand items.

My emergency money will need to be rebuilt because who knows what the future holds.

I've discovered that regardless of how much money one makes, one can also live a happy life when properly planning. I am also extremely grateful for my side business, which has helped me pay off my debt and keep from going bankrupt.

For my daughters and I, there is additionally no such thing as, "I need this new thing just because I want it." We are aware of our situation, and we have turn things over a few times. It's not always easy, but our lives will get back on track. However, I don't think we will ever go back to spending the way we used to. We are much more focused on saving for the future now!"

———

Three Tips to Prepare for the Worst

As you can see, losing your job could be an actual situation, in the uncertain times we live in.

Tip 1: Setup an Emergency Fund

An emergency fund is usually 3-to-6-months' worth of living expenses saved on the side. Margaret, however, decided to save one year's worth of living expenses because she knew it would take more time for her to get a new job at her age. Decide today to put a small amount into the fund until you reach your 3-to-6-month goal. The amount of money could be as little as $10 a month, don't stop paying into your fund until your 3 to 6 months are fully paid.

Wouldn't it be fantastic to know you have a support system that allows you to sleep comfortably? An emergency fund reduces a serious life crisis to a minor inconvenience. In other words, a buffer that separates you from a catastrophic event. How do you determine if 3 or 6 months is enough?

Well, contemplate how easy or how difficult it would be to replace a job position such as yours if you were asked to leave. According to 45% of job searchers, it is harder now to find employment than it was before the pandemic started (ResumeBuilder, 2023).

Half of these in-demand job seekers also believe that the present employment market is more competitive than it was prior to COVID-19.

If You Use the Emergency Fund

There is a purpose for this fund, and it's to be used in emergencies. So, please don't feel guilty or afraid to use your emergency fund when you need it, but don't be tempted to use it to increase your living standards.

A well-known finance expert and radio personality, Dave Ramsey, said, "If you use your emergency fund for an emergency, that's what it's there for" (Ramsey Solutions, 2022).

But that means you took a step back, and you're going to have to fill it back up, and then you'll to have to move back on. That's okay, in any case, that's what it's for. That's the rhythm of life" (Ramsey Solutions, 2022).

Your protective plan is similar to the insulation used when building a house. Your pipes might need to be protected with pipe insulation, which keeps them warm in the winter and stops them from freezing. This will also keep your pipes from cracking and leaking.

Drywall is used to build ceilings, walls, and design concepts, such as architectural peculiarities and eaves. This material is highly robust, simple, and quick to install, therefore, it only needs minor repairs when it breaks. However, leaking pipes create disaster as water will destroy the drywall.

Electrical insulation prevents electricity from arcing or sparking, which lowers the danger of injury, fire, as well as other electrical hazards. These small components are equally vital to other electrical equipment as the reliability of these complete electrical wires in a house depends on the insulation.

Tip 2: Become Debt Free

It's a necessary evil to chip away quicker at debt so that you can achieve your goals. Whether it's avoiding new credit to lower your borrowing costs or simply paying off your debt, these positive situations will help to remove debt quicker. Below are five ways to examine your repayment options for a debt-free lifestyle:

- Don't pay the minimum; if you can, pay more.

- Pay the account/s often and more than once a month.

- Always pay the most expensive loan first—reduce the highest interest rate.

- Pay the smallest loan off and create a snowball effect.

- Keep track of your bills, and set payments to autopay, so you never forget to pay on time.

If you start to feel pressured or stuck and think your income will stay pretty much the same when paying the loans, re-evaluate which of your wants you can give up to make your budget work.

Small payments and their interest add up! There is another option; some firms help to consolidate many high-interest debts, loans, or credit cards within one new loan. This is potentially organized with a reduced interest rate, and loan consolidation will help you pay off debt much quicker.

Tip 3: Avoid Loans When Possible

Avoid taking out loans but understand that they can be used as a necessary evil sometimes as avoiding them is not always possible. For instance, with today's college tuition rate, it's nearly impossible for some to get the education they need to open better working opportunities without taking out a loan. Remember to consider your borrowing costs while choosing a new loan or reorganizing your present debts.

While extending the loan's length or terms, your loan has the potential to lower its monthly payments; you may also wind up paying more in interest overall, bringing your total payments up.

Try to take loans as a last resort and only when necessary. For example, it's not necessary to take out a loan to pay for a luxury living room set, but it maybe for fixing your roof to avoid mold.

Always stop to ask yourself, is it critical? Do I actually need a new car because the one I have is unreliable, and I need a safe way to get to work in the morning? Or do I just want a new car? Is there other transportation available? Take a loan out for a car to cover the difference after selling your old car, but don't get the most expensive car in the lot. Look for quality that you can afford.

Evaluate Your Normal Spending Plan

Periodically reviewing your finances is a smart idea, especially if you have a large purchase such as a new car, or house or if your income or expenses has changed significantly. In times like these, it is essential to see how much money you are spending, and that will be thanks to your regular budget.

Fortunately, most of the knowledge you are looking for is readily available. Follow these guidelines when evaluating your finances to make sure you choose wisely and plan for the future.

When calculating your costs, the most effective approach to achieving this would be to keep a record of your monthly spending. Look at the resources provided by evaluating your checking account when you download debit or credit card bills or use your phone to capture receipts. This will simply keep track of what you are spending.

Decide which expenses are variable and which are fixed, meaning they won't fluctuate monthly, such as car payments, rent, and maybe your insurance payments. Check your costs on groceries and entertainment. Calculate your monthly expense using a three-month average system.

Separate Your Expenses

Make decisions on what to keep, what to reduce, and which items to get rid of. Ask yourself questions and find ways to bring down specific expenses. You can also get the disparity by adding your year's revenue and expenses and then subtracting the total expense.

Review Your Goals

Cost goals aim to cut costs while maintaining a high level of quality and good service.

Create a Profit

Earnings, focused on the overall, are frequently used to support profit goals. or instance, a household will profit more significantly while increasing income and reducing expenses. Give yourself some leeway; save any additional funds and reassess your goals after three months.

Prompt

- Write down your monthly expenses for the duration of 3-to-6 months' and then subtract any wants, such as eating out and getting your nails done. It may be easiest to do this in a spreadsheet.

    o Add your loan payments to that monthly expense.

- Set a 1-year timeline. What needs to happen in your budget to allow you to save 3 to 6 months' worth of savings?

- If you are finding this book to be helpful, I'd really appreciate it if you left your feedback at the reviews page of where you bought this book. The more reviews mean the more likely someone else will find *Personal Finance for Young Adults*.

Chapter 5

Maintain It To Sustain It

"The only way you can predict the future is to build it" by
Alan Kay.

With any property, there is always regular maintenance; it could be mowing the lawn, fixing a garage door, re-hanging a wall unit cupboard, or cleaning out a gutter. It's an ongoing situation, keeping up the maintenance. Whether you built a tiny home or a mansion, maintenance will ultimately determine whether your house and property stay in good condition for years.

As a homeowner, you will need to make some repairs. However, keeping up with regular maintenance chores will help you avoid more severe issues and inevitably save you a lot of money. Regular house inspections can also help you save a lot of money. For instance, the average cost of a new roof is

$6,800, but minor repairs only cost a couple hundred dollars.

This is similar to tweaking problem areas concerning our day-to-day living regarding bad habits that creep in. It may be an extra pound you gained over the weekend or that crazy tab you racked up at the bar when you overdid the "good times."

Now that you have a budget appropriate for your income and goals, your finances should start looking healthier. A budget allows you to live sustainably when you have an income, but what happens when that income stops?

The moment has come to adopt a proactive mindset. Dial into a long-term plan and change your life as you reach your future goals.

Three Tips to Build That Future You Want

There are three main hurdles to jump through when building money over time: generating finances, saving money, and investing, which all work towards helping you accumulate funds. Although it may seem simple, these stages are among the most important for those getting started.

It would help if you broke free of the mindset of impossibilities. Consider using a portion of what you are saving to invest, whether 3%, 5%, or 10% of your monthly savings, to help you maintain the lifestyle you have and desire when you retire.

You have probably seen graphs demonstrating how a small sum of financial gain is saved consistently and encouraged to compound over time, eventually evolving into substantial sums. The graphs are accurate; $100 a month is $36,000 over 30 years, but investing it can generate more than you imagine.

The two main methods of earning income are well-earned and earning passive income. Earned money is achieved from your job, whereas passive income is derived from investments. Below, let's focus on the three building blocks:

Tip 1: Start Investing Today

Investing refers to buying stocks, real estate, and other valuable items with the intention of that money appreciating over time. This will generate money or capital gains through the investment.

If you have invested wisely, capital gains or income will offer a return. In a broader sense, investment can also mean devoting time or resources to a project to better your quality of life. It costs nothing to open an investment account and only $1 to get started.

Pros:

- There is no charge in selling investments.

- There is exposure in ETFs.

- Roundups: In addition to adding figures.

- Cash Back: You can receive cash back when shopping with certain companies.

Cons:

- Unlike investing in a Roth or traditional IRA, there is no tax strategy.

- High fees on small balances.

Stocks and Bonds

Whenever you purchase stock, you become a minor shareholder in the business you bought stock in. Right now, you have gained the upside potential of its share price and any dividends it may pay.

When you purchase a bond, the issuer pledges to return your funds and interest at a later time. Bonds are again considered less risky than stocks, despite their lower upside potential. Bond-rating organizations award letter grades to illustrate that some bonds are more volatile than others.

Mutual Funds

Mutual funds are collections of securities, frequently consisting of stocks, bonds, or a mix of the two. Shares in mutual funds give you access to the entire pool. The risk of mutual funds varies as well, and this will depend on the investments that are taken.

Any investor should look to diversify their investment portfolio. As investments behave differently depending on the time of year, they also depend on the economy. For example, bonds may offer strong returns if the stock market is experiencing a losing stretch. If stock "A" is struggling, stock "C" can skyrocket.

Mutual funds offer some built-in diversification. Additionally, investing in both a bond fund and a stock fund, or many stock funds and multiple bond funds, for example, as opposed to just one of each will result in better diversification.

Asset allocation is a concept that is strongly related to diversification. It entails the choice based on risk and other considerations, such as a portion of your portfolio you want to invest in, and each specific asset has a category or type of securities.

Tools — Betterment, Acorns, or Robinhood for Beginners

The word investing is easier said than done, so much so that entrepreneurs found ways to make it easier and helped millions like you and me by creating tools such as the following listed below. You can start investing today without digging deeper into what stocks, bonds or even mutual funds are or feeling any pressure to keep up with the market to know when to buy and sell. You could choose to only work with only one of the accounts below or diversify into all of them, if you don't think it will overwhelm you.

Acorns

Acorns is ideal for investors that want long-term, broad portfolios that don't need much maintenance.

Investing and saving are made simple at Acorns when using automatic roundups. All you do is link your bank account to Acorns, and whenever you spend money on your card, Acorns will round it up and invest the rest. For example, if you spent $5,75 on your card, they would round it up to $6 and invest the $0.25. This way, you barely feel it as the money comes out. You could also invest additional money on a one-time or regular basis. Below are the pros and cons to look out for:

To Open an Account and Start Investing

It's free to open an account, and only takes $5 to begin investing.

Selling Investments

There is no charge when selling your investments, but the broker will take $35 when you close your account.

Exposure

Great exposure via stocks; there are bonds in domestic and international areas. They also have a linked ETF with both REIT and Bitcoin on board.

Roundups

In addition to adding lump sums to your investments, Acorns enables you to round up your purchases made with linked credit or debit cards and then sweeps the change into a computer-managed investment portfolio. You can setup your account with a lump sum and/or roundups.

Cash Back

Shopping with companies that invest in you can help you make money that will expand. Acorns offers cash back at over 450 retailers.

No Tax Strategy

Unlike many of its competitors, Acorns does not offer a tax strategy.

High Fees on Small Balance

Acorns can, however, have high fees on small account balances due to their pricing structure.

Robinhood

Robinhood is better for those that wish to begin their journey with a basic asset set.

Robinhood offers free trades in stock options, ETFs, and cryptocurrencies. It also matches 1% of IRA contributions; the account minimum is $0. Robinhood doesn't diversify into bonds and mutual funds.

To Open an Account and Start Investing

It costs nothing to open an account and to invest.

Selling Investments

Matching funds can be (confiscated) when withdrawing from IRAs if you close your account in less than 5 years.

Exposure

The web platform is basic when meeting the investor's needs. Charges of $5 a month will be paid when receiving data such as level 11 marketing.

Retirement Accounts

Robinhood introduced individual retirement accounts (IRAs) with a 1% match in December 2022. The 1% match on contributions is a feature that distinguishes Robinhood IRAs from any other retirement plan. This is a first for a sponsored nonemployer-retirement fund.

Costs

Robinhood is a bargain broker, and although a few other brokerages may have more product variety, it offers among the lowest costs in the market.

It's also quite simple to use. In fact, some have claimed that the "Streamlined User Interface" has made sophisticated trading techniques, such as options trading, too approachable for novice users.

However, the simplified interface is quite useful if all you want to do is invest in stocks or save for retirement.

It also offers free cryptocurrency trading, making it unique among stock brokerages. Unfortunately, that brilliance somewhat tarnishes when you contrast Robinhood's crypto products with those of pure-play crypto brokerages.

Additionally, there is no cryptocurrency support for

Robinhood IRAs, and there is no access to IPOs: Robinhood, however, enables consumers to participate in a first-ever public offering (IPO).

Reliability

Although Robinhood's customer care has improved noticeably, it still needs to catch up. Regulators have accused Robinhood of deceiving clients, which resulted in significant fines. The company has also been criticized for sudden outages and trade limitations amid market volatility.

Betterment

Betterment investors only require a little maintenance and value a simple user interface. It's ideal for beginner investors that don't have much capital for deposits. These are often customers who favor investing with a goal base in mind.

Betterment is the undisputed leader among robo-advisors, with the following two primary services:

- Betterment Premium costs a minimum of $100 and an annual fee of 0–40%. However, it offers unlimited access to a phone regarding financial planners.

- Betterment Digital offers an automated management portfolio for $10 to open an account and invest.

Betterment's goal-oriented tools and useful tax

techniques will help many investors. The Premium plan or a stand-alone guidance package can give users access to human consultants.

There are many portfolio customization choices and a highly affordable yearly management fee of 0.25%. The money goes into fractional shares and is absorbed into an entire investment.

There is no automatic access to an advisor. Regardless of whether a person possesses an account, anybody could purchase a $299 advice bundle that includes an advisor with a consultation.

Cash Account

The cash account has no charge, no minimum required, and it's an unrestricted transaction. You can bank up to $1,000,000 in FDIC insurance coverage. It also has a function that allows users to store money for various goals in distinct buckets. It also has the option of a checking account with a cash-back-paying with a debit card that covers ATM and foreign transaction costs.

Betterment's Shortcomings

Betterment does not offer direct indexing, although the company does offer tax-loss harvesting. Betterment falls short with rival Wealthfront, as they offer direct indexing for no charge on accounts worth $100,000 or more.

These three building blocks – stocks, bonds, and mutual funds - are complex, but anyone can get started today with the right beginner tools.

Investments Do the Work for You

Investing may give you a second source of income, finance your retirement, or pull you out of a tight financial spot. Above all, investments increase your money, enabling you to reach your financial goals and gradually boosting your purchasing power. Remember, they are not always quick-win situations and work best if you are in it for the long run.

Exchange-Traded Funds

Similar to mutual funds, ETFs are investment pools. One significant distinction is that the shares are traded instead of bought and sold through a company. They also impose less. Additionally, you can purchase funds through a brokerage with equities and bonds.

Certificates of Deposits

This type of savings account is where the financial institution rewards an interest in exchange for holding a specified sum of money for a predetermined length of time. You will receive an initially invested amount plus interest when you redeem it.

Real Estate

Real estate involves owning any immovable property giving you a stake in the land, house, or both. It also includes the resources on the land, such as water, minerals, plants, or crops.

Buy REIT

They have large amounts of commercial real estate property available for rent. REIT is investing in real estate as a well-acclaimed company. They are frequently compared to mutual funds due to their propensity for paying substantial dividends.

Investors can automatically reinvest dividends to increase the value of their investment if they do not use it as a regular income. Some are not publicly traded, while others are exchanged on the market, similar to the exchange of stocks.

Given that nontraded is made difficult when it comes to selling and may also be challenging to evaluate, this fact significantly impacts the level of risk you assume. In general, novice investors should be cautious about risks and stick to publicly traded companies that buy through brokerage companies.

Online Real Estate Investing Platforms

These real estate investment platforms interact with investors who want to fund projects with either debt or equity. Investors take on a lot of risk in paying a fee to the platform in the hope of a monthly or quarterly amount in exchange.

These are unstable and illiquid investments that create a presumptuous mindset. Similar to many real estate situations, the catch comes with selling the property quickly, as with stock. The problem is that making money always requires a person to spend money. Many of these platforms are only accessible to accredited investors.

Except for a principal residence, investors are financially screened to see if they meet the requirements to participate in transactions. Investors have to be worth a net value of $1 million or more and collect an annual income of more than $200,000 or $300,000, depending on whether a spouse participates in the transactions.

The Securities and Exchange Commission is responsible for calculating these numbers. Individuals who are unable to achieve that threshold could consider Fundrise and RealtyMogul.

Invest in Rental Properties

Purchase a whole investment property to rent out. When

moving in this direction, monetary gain is significant; find a property where the total costs are less than the rent you can charge.

You could also consider hiring a property manager/company to handle renting out the units, any maintenance requests, and collecting payments. You could also manage these tasks yourself to retain more of your profit. In that case, you will learn and gain a great deal from the business and have experience when purchasing other properties.

Investing in an entire property alone can feel daunting, which is why Corey Ashton Walters built his company. Here, a company that purchases vacation rentals allows everyday investors like yourself to contribute with as little as $100 and earn quarterly returns.

Community Housing

A few years ago, I met a woman who told me she lived in a community house a block away from the university. I looked interested, and she told me she loved it there because of the sense of community the owner built.

A student's father bought a run-down property and slowly renovated it. The son stayed in the refurbished cottage that is detached from the house. When parts of the house were completed, it was sealed off from the ongoing renovation and was made available for rent. Students jumped at the offer as university accommodation is so expensive.

Eventually, all eight rooms were rented out. Not only did it wind up paying for itself, but it also funded the son's tuition. The son graduated after several years and was given the keys to the house. This little business has become a gold mine.

Consider Flipping Properties

There is so much media coverage about flipping properties, especially on HGTV. People source and buy the worst house in the nicest area, fix it, and flip it for a massive profit. The idea is to purchase a home with cash and take out a loan for the repairs. The property is undervalued and in need of TLC, and then restore it on a budget and flip it for a profit. The tactic is challenging and not as easy as it looks, especially if you do not have any experience with home repairs. Hiring a contractor is the safest option, but it may rack up lots of debt.

Not everyone is gifted at construction and interior design, and one has to consider the hidden costs. Given the present greater cost of building materials and the mortgage interest loan rates, it's not as viable as it was in previous years. Yet, there is still money to be made, if you are willing and able to!

If you are not sure how to renovate a home, you should

find an experienced partner to help guide you or take up a smaller renovation project first to see if you can handle it. If you don't have enough funds, you could also offer your time to someone else flipping homes to learn how they do it.

The other risk is that you could lose money if there is more severe damage than you initially projected or if you have to hold on to the property for too long because it won't sell. Now, in this case, a mortgage cost will add unwanted pressure.

By residing in the house while it is being renovated, you could reduce that risk because you don't have a separate mortgage or rent payment to make. This will work, provided that most of the upgrades are cosmetic and you don't struggle with dust allergies.

Rent Out a Room

A similar arrangement would enable people to continue enjoying property value benefits while significantly reducing their housing costs. Younger folks may find it easier to afford a mortgage payment by renting out to roommates. In this case, consider trying a website like Airbnb if you are still determining whether this is something you can personally do long-term.

You don't have to take on a long-term tenant, as Airbnb at least somewhat prescreens potential tenants. The company guarantees security with protection against damage, through their Host Damage Protection program.

When comparing an enterprise regarding the renting out of one room, in comparison to the glorious idea of real estate investing, room renting sounds approachable since you can rent out a room if you have one to make some extra income.

Invest in What you Enjoy

Former NBA basketball star, Shaquille O'Neal, said that he said he received his inspiration from Jeff Bezos (Amazon founder and CEO). As he heard Jeff say, he will only invest based on feelings of whether it will change people's lives.

O'Neal deviates from the general trend of professional athletes who experience financial difficulty after retirement when leaving the league in 2011. O'Neal told *The Wall Street Journal* that he invested his money in ways that he found appealing. He also said he gets that feeling in his gut and knows it's right.

"If something comes across my desk, and I don't believe in it, I don't even look at it," O'Neal told *The Wall Street Journal*. "Whenever I do business, it's not about the money. I like donuts...Krispy Kreme is a fabulous donut. I was introduced to it in college and have been in love with it ever since" (Hernbroth, 2019). He claimed that although his investment in the Krispy Kreme doughnut chain is his favorite, Google is by far his best investment.

When picking an investment, invest in things you believe in and personally use so that if it doesn't pan out, you aren't as bummed about it. It's essential to do your homework before throwing hard-earned cash at it (Hernbroth, 2019).

Tip 2: Setup your Retirement Account

Retirement is the conclusion of one's employment, busy work, or occupation. Another way to semi-retire is to work fewer hours or fewer days. When people age or are physically unable to perform their profession, they retire. A retirement fund is the cushion that allows them to have an income once their work stops paying them. Here are a few retirement plan options.

401(k) — Employee Sponsored

The setup and upkeep of the 401(k) retirement are simple when your company offers an automatic payroll deduction option. The retirement plan administrator, a different financial institution, oversees statements, disclosures, and updates. The 401(k) derives its name from the "Internal Revenue Code" passage that allows employees to contribute.

Make contributions large enough to qualify for any free

money your employer provides through the corporate match. If your employer will partially match your contribution, this is known as gratuitous cash. The maximum contributions to a 401(k) are more significant than those to an IRA fund. So, it's advisable to do the 401(k)-retirement fund if you have an option.

Your taxable income is decreased by the employee contributions that go onto a non-Roth plan for a year. Yet, you will be taxed on retirement withdrawals due to that first tax benefit.

There is no immediate tax benefit with regard to a Roth 401(k) as contributions are made with after-tax funds. In contrast, retirement withdrawals from the account are tax-free.

Contrary to the Roth IRA, the Roth 401(k) has no restrictions on your income. Below are the fundamental drawbacks:

- You have fewer alternatives than you would with an IRA since the investment possibilities available through employer-sponsored retirement plans are restricted to specific funds.

- High administrative and management costs may gradually reduce the earnings on your investments.

- In order to contribute to this plan, new hires may be

subject to a waiting period that can last anywhere from 30 to 90 days after the employment sign-up date.

- An employee may only become the owner of an employer contribution after a predetermined period of time, following a vesting schedule.

The 401(k) and a SIMPLE IRA

The SIMPLE is a reasonably good alternative if you own a midsize business with less than 100 employees since it is simple to setup, and the accounts are in the possession of your employees.

One stipulation is that early withdrawals are subject to the same taxation before the age of 59 and 6 months. This is because a 401(k) or IRA is meant to be used for retirement, and taking them out early, signals a different use, which will inquire a 10% penalty. However, the 10% penalty increases to 25% if you withdraw money from a SIMPLE IRA during the first two years of joining.

This implies that there is no profitable way to roll over a SIMPLE into another retirement plan during those two years. A 401(k) variant for a SIMPLE operates similarly but permits participants to borrow money from their accounts. This variant can be more expensive to setup and calls for greater administrative monitoring.

IRA—Individual Retirement Account

Retirement distributions are not subject to tax withholdings.

- Contributions may be withdrawn at any moment without penalties, but investment earnings are tax-free.

- Based on one's income, eligibility to donate gradually disappears.

- It only provides tax savings when the retirement tax rate is greater.

- You must be earning money to contribute.

A Setup Plan if Your Company Doesn't Offer a 401(k)

A retirement savings plan is provided to almost half of employees at businesses, with less than 100 workers. If you are self-employed or work for a small business or both, you may have access to a distinct selection of retirement plans.

A few are based on IRAs, while others are effectively small 401(k) plans. Profit-sharing programs are another kind of defined contribution program. It's far more important to save money when you are on your own, as opposed to an employee who might have access to a 401(k).

The optimal plan would be to determine an amount

intended for saving annually. After that, choose where to invest that money.

Traditional or Roth IRA

Individual retirement accounts are best suited for newcomers. Roths are the newcomers to the realm of retirement money. The Roth IRA was established in 1998 and is named after the late Delaware senator William Roth. This plan was followed by Roth 401(k) in 2006. The Roth is an effective retirement option that established a tax-free income stream.

You can convert your former 401(k) into an IRA if you change your work situation or want to launch your own business. The 2023 IRA contribution cap is $6,500 ($7,500 if you are over 50).

Traditional IRA contributions are tax deductible. Yet, Roth IRA contributions are not immediately tax-deductible, but withdrawals made from retirement contributions are tax-free.

These retirement plans are private. For instance, if you have staff, the employees can open a fund with their own IRA accounts. This is the most straightforward approach for independent contractors to begin saving for retirement.

You can use this plan if you have employees or not; it's

also easy as there are no specific filing requirements. Choosing which kind of IRA account to open might be more of a challenge. This retirement offers distinctions between regular and Roth IRAs accounts.

When considering that you are starting a new business for yourself. It's understandable that it will take time before it makes a substantial profit. In this case, the Roth IRA's tax treatment might be your best option, allowing you to withdraw tax-free funds during retirement. The only drawback is your overall tax rate will probably be a bit higher.

For 2023, the maximum contribution permitted is $66,000 with a catch-up of $7,500 in payments, or 100% of earned income, whichever works out to be less. You may also contribute up to 25% of your salary, in your capacity as an employer.

There is a specific rule regarding sole entrepreneurs and single-member LLCs. The rule states you may contribute up to 25% of your net self-employment income, which is your net profit. This is less than the self-employment tax you paid on half of the plan contributions you made for yourself.

SIMPLE IRA

This plan is best for larger companies that employ 100 employees. Maximum contributions are:

- $15,500 which is payable from 2023, this amount was $14,000 in 2022, with a $3,500 catch-up payment in 2023. $3,000 was paid in 2022 if the person who contributed was older than 50.

- The sum of contributions to an employer plan cannot exceed $22,500 in 2023; it was $20,500 in 2022.

Traditional SIMPLE IRA contributions are tax-deductible, but retirement withdrawals are taxed. Employee account contributions are deductible as a company expense. It is now permitted to combine your Roth contributions, passed in 2023, according to legislation in December 2022.

SEP IRA isn't responsible for all the contribution costs, and salary deferral is one-way employees might contribute. However, businesses are often required to provide either fixed contributions of 2% to every qualifying employee or they can match contributions to the employee's account of up to 3%.

If you choose the latter, an employee does not have to contribute for a business owner to contribute. The cap on factor contribution payments is:

- $330,000 in 2023, and it was $305,000 in 2022.

Opening a SIMPLE requires more paperwork than a conventional IRA and follows a similar approach to opening a SEP IRA. The SIMPLE is a reasonably good alternative if you own a midsize business with less than 100 employees since it is simple to setup, and the employees hold the accounts.

Yet, the SIMPLE IRA contribution limitations are far smaller than those of a SEP IRA or a solo 401(k). If you have a lot of employees, you might have to make required payments to the employee accounts, which may be expensive. Below are some details on the differences between a 401(k) and a SIMPLE IRA.

Comparing IRAs and 401(k)

With a 401(k), employers may provide matching funds that are simple to setup and maintain. To add contributions to your retirement plan, most companies offer an automatic payroll deduction option. Be sure to check in with your Human Resources department for more information.

This is when an employer matches a percentage of the contribution. (This is called gratuitous cash!)

The maximum contribution to a 401(k) is greater than those made to an IRA. Your taxable income is decreased by employee contributions (to non-Roth plans) for the year. You will have to pay taxes on your retirement withdrawals due to that first tax benefit.

On the other hand, Roth 401(k) contributions are made with after-tax funds, so there is no immediate tax benefit.

Employer-sponsored retirement plans only offer a select few funds as investment alternatives; this gives you fewer choices compared to an IRA.

The earnings on your investments may be gradually reduced by high management and administrative costs.

There may be a waiting period before new employees are permitted to make contributions to a plan (e.g., 30 to 90 days of employment). Here's how to choose between investing in a 401(k) or an IRA if you have a finite amount of money set aside for retirement.

- A vesting schedule for employer contributions may apply, in which case, funds are only made available to employees after a predetermined period of employment.

- Contrary to the Roth IRA, the Roth 401(k) has no restrictions on income.

Fundamental Drawbacks

Participants may fund both standard and Roth 401(k) accounts if their employer offers both. The combined annual cap was $20,500 in 2022 and $22,500 in 2023 (or $27,000 for those who are 50 years and older).

Investment Distribution Date

Unlike a Roth IRA, a Roth 401(k) requires you to begin drawing minimum distributions at the age of 73; Roth IRAs have no requirement for withdrawals until the customer's passing. Yet their beneficiaries are still governed by the RMD regulations.

Things to Consider

If you quit your position or are made redundant, take your retirement fund with you, and set it up as an IRA fund. This will stop you from losing money on penalties. You could take your existing account to either Vanguard or Fidelity, and they will roll it over for you. This is a solution since retirement money is taxed when taken too early or moved to your new company's 401(k).

There are few exceptions, but in general, the IRS's 10% tax levy is charged as a penalty on early withdrawals when a retirement plan is moved from a standard 401(k). This tax aims to promote savings in participation with the employer-sponsored retirement plan for the period of retirement.

There is no legal prohibition against simply liquidating the entire account if you suddenly require cash for an unanticipated expense. These expenses can be withdrawn to meet the needs of a beneficiary, spouse, or dependent. One of the most common ways to save for retirement is through an Individual Retirement Account (IRA).

In addition to saving money for the future, you also receive a significant tax break from the government. An IRA is a beautiful fund to start with. If you are trying to finance your retirement as quickly as possible, set one up online in just a few minutes.

Investing in the financial markets is considered to be one of the most effective and trustworthy ways to build a nest egg. Still, you may want a brokerage account or robo-advisor to do so:

- You can pick your own investments with a brokerage account comprising individual stocks, bonds, stock funds, or more.

- You might want to open your own account or have someone else do it for you, like a broker; you might also want to do something in between, like getting a financial advisor.

- Your portfolio will be created by a robo-advisor who will choose the funds and distribute your assets in accordance with your risk factor and the time you have to invest.

With a 401(k), money is pre-taxed when used to establish

the account. Therefore, you must pay income tax on the amount you removed from it. So, suppose you take an early withdrawal from your retirement account because of an emergency. In that case, the money will be considered income and fall into another tax bracket.

This might be avoided if you prove that you have certain hardship distributions or significant life milestones that must be covered. Below are a few exceptions to this rule:

- paying for college

- buying a house

- emergency expenses

The majority of 401(k) members must have proof and abide by this legislation. There are also a few other exceptions when being taxed, and one is if a person becomes disabled, but that is only allowed after the age of 55 years or if the individual has worked in the public sector.

Best Accounts to Open and Why

Charles Schwab excels at the essential aspects of brokerage, a discount broker licensed in the U.S. and governed by the SEC and FINRA. Investing trade in stocks and ETFs is free at Charles Schwab. Its research is of the highest caliber and includes a wide range of tools, such as trade suggestions and comprehensive fundamental data.

Customer services respond quickly and with useful information. When investing, it is a wise decision, especially for novice investors. The reason is that you can start investing with as little as $100. They also have a longstanding reputation for reliable service and friendliness. Schwab can handle your request from stocks, bonds, ETFs, and CDs within your IRA.

They also provide tens of thousands of mutual funds without any transaction costs. Additionally, this broker gets their claim to fame as being consistently ranked among the best in the sector thanks to commission-free trades and responsive client support.

If you want to be more actively involved, there are more options, and one is to utilize StreetSmart Edge. This is Schwab's leading trading platform, so get started and trade.

Tip 3: Building Multiple Sources of Income

Having multiple sources of income means you have a backup plan. This is to ensure you are prepared if your primary source of money disappears. Having various sources of income reduces some of the financial concerns or stress that losing a job might cause.

Passive Income

The idea with passive income is to earn a consistent income with as little effort as possible. Unfortunately, passive income generation is not a sit-back and get-rich-quick scheme.

Starting can be challenging, but there are ways and means to achieve a passive income. When passive income is consistently maintained, it can become lucrative in generating income, and you can accumulate significant wealth over time.

For example, building a blog or an app requires time and money to get off the ground. If you persevere and manage what you are given, you will eventually be able to make money while you sleep.

Social Media

Have you seen the families on tik tok that show you their day, the people who create dancing videos, or even how to work out at the gym safely? That's called influencer marketing; they gain traction then companies seek them out to create ads for them for a significant fee to the influencer, but way less for the big brand-named company. This generation has been fortunate to witness technology grow and develop.

Check out other exciting ways to make passive income work for you:

- rent out practical objects

- launch a blog or a YouTube channel

- offer digital goods

- implement affiliate marketing

- promote ads on your car

- sign up to rent your car out

- be an uber or lyft driver

- purchase and sell stock

People have a lot of material possessions, and are constantly looking for inexpensive ways to store them. What could be simpler than getting people to pay you to store their stuff? Think of keeping their belongings for them if you have room in the garage or basement.

Make sure their belongings are protected and secure. To get started, look into sites like Neighbor, Store At My House, or iStoreit. These services make use of a person's interior or outdoor area and help you bring in an additional income.

Additionally, people will pay more if you have a larger area to rent out. For example, if you have a barn, garage, or a simple carport that can be used for storing expensive toys, cars, boats, campers, horses, and other vehicles, you could make a decent amount of passive money.

Prompt

Write down the answers to the questions below and reflect on them.

- Consider the lifestyle you want to lead after retirement.

  - Do you intend on traveling a lot?

  - Do you prefer a peaceful existence and long for that in your current residence?

  - Do you intend to reside with your kids?

- Now run the numbers and see what you need to earn to keep your current standard of living.

  - Could you live the life you desire if you reduce your monthly salary by a certain percentage?

- Then, go setup one investment account that best suits your needs, whether it's opening an account or researching the price of real estate.

  - Sign up right away. If $1 is all you have, that's fine; anything is better than nothing.

Chapter 6

Share The Wealth

"There is no exercise better for the heart than reaching down and lifting people up" by John Holmes.

In the same way, you would host a housewarming party when you finish building your home; you can host a dinner party with your girlfriends to teach and learn how they manage their finances. Don't be stingy with the information you have received; their success does not detract from yours.

The Road to Success Doesn't Come Easily

I appreciate all the effort my mom put into raising me. Yet, I had a rocky start to life even though my immigrant parents worked hard to give me what I had. My mom taught me to take risks and invest in myself; this helped me take advantage of multiple opportunities.

When faced with the decision to take out $100k+ in student debt to go to a world-renowned university, I was overwhelmed. Still, I know that it was the right decision for me. Yes, I have been overwhelmed by the amount, but I am confident it was worth the investment. This reminds me of a well-known personality, Milton Hershey.

Did you know that Milton founded three other candy businesses before Hershey's was founded? At the time, he was utterly unknown, and he had just gone through a setback after being fired from an apprenticeship in a printing company.

He again faced a disaster as he witnessed each of the three ventures fail. Yet Hershey refused to give up because he believed in himself and his passion. He only had enough funds to have one last effort to establish Lancaster Caramel Company, and it soon began to experience great success.

The formation of the Hershey Company came to life, and it grew to be one of the world's most recognizable names in the field of milk chocolate. He saw his dream of providing chocolates to the masses become a reality only because he stayed committed (Mr. Great Motivation, 2022).

Regardless of how many of these setbacks you have had, take encouragement from stories like these. Some failures may appear to end your journey, but it's not. Don't give up; come on, give it another go.

Bear in mind that innumerable successful people in the world only achieved their goals because they decided to push past the unavoidable gloom of failure. Sharing stories and spreading what you have learned will help others start their journey in building their financial mindset.

———

Three Tips for Sharing the Wealth

Did you know that one quarter of all married couples in America have no knowledge about their spouse's financial situation? An astoundingly 15% of couples could not describe their partner's employment position or status.

Information from a Fidelity study indicated that 1,713 couples have very little information on their partner's finances. Around 40% of American couples couldn't accurately determine how much their partner makes.

Participants that took part in the yearly "Couples and Money" study were subjected to a financial inquiry as a married couple. Committed couples, who had been together for 25 years or more, had trouble identifying their partner's salaries. Even though 71% of couples claim to converse "extremely well," and 1 in 4 claim to speak "amazingly well" about money matters (Vega, 2021).

According to Fidelity, even though they are given a

choice of a wider money range for participants to choose from while guessing, only 1 out of 10 people could guess or come close to determining their partner's pay.

Many couples are reluctant to open up and share about money, even with their partners. Individuals don't always make time to discuss their finances as they claim that life is too busy.

The reason may be that most people who are questioned about their finances consider it insulting or repulsive. You will pick this up quickly, as awkward pauses, embarrassing grins, or a forced cough often follow questions.

The finance topic has joined the risky subjects to discuss, including religion, politics, and sex. But why is money talk so taboo? In what ways do folks differ in their approaches to money?

Tip 1: End the Taboo

Our values and views are embodied in our culture. They teach us that life's best experiences involve a certain pride in family, one's country, allegiance, rivalry, kindness, or material achievement.

These cultural precepts serve as the foundation for social norms and proper conduct. Every time someone behaves in a way that deviates from the "norm," it influences the members of society. This is seen as someone who has dared to cross the boundary line.

Tell me now, what justifies the taboo against discussing money, then? One reason is the wrong or lousy notion that prosperity is a measure of value. Is there a notion that our worth or importance increases with our income?

As a result, questioning anyone about how much money they earn at work is similar to asking them where they belong in social standings. If I make more money than you, I must be superior. But did you know that when sharing your income, you have an opportunity to stomp out inequality for women?

People don't like to share because of culture and generational norms. An example of this is *Jantelagen*, a widely used Nordic code that is utilized throughout Scandinavia. The phrase, used initially by novelist Aksel Sandemose, is a standard way of behavior in Norway, Sweden, Norway, and Denmark (Thomson, 2022).

It's the notion that you shouldn't ever consider yourself to be superior to anyone else and that it's undesirable to put yourself in a situation in which you could be thought of in that way. Scandinavian societies, as a result, have very private opinions on money and assets.

Based on a different theory discussing money and riches might help us resolve whatever issues we may be experiencing.

The following is what author Joe Pinsker states in a piece for *The Atlantic* about Americans and their reasoning when they avoid speaking about money matters.

He said, "…taboos around money—among haves and have-nots alike—exert a sort of stabilizing force, blurring how much people actually have and giving them one fewer reason to be upset with their place in society" (Thomson, 2022).

Guilt, or perhaps the pressure of consciousness, in knowing they are successful and leading a simpler life. This fact causes anxiety that results from people discussing money.

Ultimately, addressing money can cause the majority to feel uneasy, particularly when these discrepancies are apparent. Whenever a coworker, for instance, pulls another shift to provide for their family, other individuals may be embarrassed to discuss the fun they had in their new swimming pool.

Even if there is a social taboo against discussing money in most nations, this is not the case everywhere. In China, discussing wages, expenses, and the amount of your rent with colleagues and friends is often regarded as normal.

Money is not whispered about; instead, money is considered to be a happy natural aspect of life. The "red envelope," for example, is an envelope stuffed with cash given to a kid. It means good luck and is among the most popular presents to give at birthday parties.

People's inclination to talk about money also differs with age. According to studies, 71% of participants between the ages of 20 and early 30s felt comfortable discussing money matters with their peers, in contrast to 31% who are retired or close to retiring, as they felt less than agreeable when talking about money (Thomson, 2022).

Some evidence backs up the theory that our financial situation worsens when we don't discuss our finances. Making financial decisions involving your spouse creates fewer financial risks, making you less susceptible to framing (Thomson, 2022).

Framing has the propensity to make decisions according to a reaction to distinct circumstances. This significantly depends on the context in which an option is offered (or framed).

Regardless of the findings, you get to decide how much or how little you want to share, but there is no harm in sharing tips and tools. Sharing your best practices in getting where you are today can be extremely beneficial.

As we all know, knowledge is power. As a woman sharing your income can help you learn if you are making as much as your counterparts. When you realize you don't earn the same, this information enables you to gain the frustration that will motivate you to advocate for more or help you feel confident that you are being paid fairly. To get to a place where you and others feel comfortable sharing, try out these tips below:

1. Host a girls' night where everyone is relaxed.

2. In advance, tell your girlfriends that you want to use this time to help each other advance professionally. You want your friends to prepare what they want to share without being forced into it.

3. Share your story—what are you struggling with professionally?

4. Share your income when appropriate and ask others if they relate.

5. See what happens. Let the conversation flow.

6. Write down and share out the lessons or action items you are taking from this conversation.

7. If successful, keep scheduling more of theses conversations.

Tip 2: Stay Financially Free

Maintaining financial freedom even when you are wealthy means you must budget to avoid the temptation of splurging and losing everything. Take advice from people who have lived and learned and are happy to share their failures and success. One of these people is Nicolas Cage, a famous action-movie star.

The Story of Nicholas Cage's Financial Crash

Nicolas Cage overspent and lost $150 million. Cage, now valued at about $25 million, was accepting gigs everywhere to help pay off his outstanding debt. Apart from extremely expensive items, such as a jet and a $20 million yacht, he loves owning properties and houses.

Nicolas once owned 15 homes, including an $8.5 million property in Las Vegas, a $15.7 million private estate in Newport, Rhode Island, and a $25 million waterfront mansion in Newport Beach, California (Yaged, 2016).

Unfortunately, Nicolas only kept his wealth for a short time, as he wasted it away on a series of pricey and frequently bizarre acquisitions, eventually finding himself in foreclosure on several houses when payments went into arrears.

Cage suffered two blows; one was from a tight cash flow, and one was from a sharp slump in housing values. He also neglected to make his mortgage payment and left his back taxes to mount up. Here are the six situations below where we can learn through Cage's mistakes:

- Use caution when dealing with your real estate agent, learn to say no, and know the hidden costs.

- Pay off one house at a time. Always pay off your mortgage, even if you have to put off paying some other obligations due to financial issues.

- Avoid purchasing real estate, which is particularly expensive, during a housing boom.

- Don't purchase real estate without the resources to endure a potential market slump.

- Ensure you can afford the monthly payments through good and poor economic times.

- Put the house up for sale if you struggle to afford it. Contact your bank(s) when you have trouble making monthly repayments. Don't allow things to go to the point where you end up in court as Cage did.

Keep the values you have established and your finances in line. For example, if you can afford a sports car, but it's not something you value, don't consider buying it.

Tip 3: Build Generational Wealth

Generational *wealth* describes any asset a family passes on to its offspring or grandchildren. This wealth may manifest itself in various ways, such as cash, stock shares, real estate, bonds, investment funds, or stock in a family business.

Simply said, generational wealth is giving your family hope and financial freedom. You might have forgotten about creating a future for the next generations as you were preoccupied with more important situations until now.

Building generational wealth might be a low priority right now; however, you can still include it in your long-term goals. Planning for it will cost you less stress and money now than waiting until you are 50.

Look into equipping your family with information about creating start-up funds for their enterprises. This healthy situation will give them a heads-up, and they can start to invest in their future. Create a financial foundation for the generations to come, to pay it forward to those you helped bring into this world.

You have probably learned that changing the circumstances you were born into as you embark on your financial journey is difficult. It will be, but do you want to give your kids something better than you had?

If you say yes, the difficult work will be worth it! Studies indicate that in the upcoming years, a significant increase in wealth will be transferred as more adults start to consider the financial legacy they want to leave for their offspring (Get early bird, 2022).

Society is becoming more aware of how significant money provision is for the future. If you have or intend to have children, you should consider how you can help their financial prospects.

Kevin Hart said in an interview that no one wants to share their information on how they reached their success. You must beg them, and then maybe they might divulge a bit. He said it's not to say that someone will use that information; it's only adding to the value or perhaps the process of discovering their success.

A person needs to hear where the potholes are in life and how difficult it can be, and how badly a person has messed up. They need to appreciate the journey of how to work on their mental fitness; so, they can become wiser and be equipped to make better decisions.

Kevin said that those who have made it out of a certain poverty-stricken environment must go back and help others who can relate to that person and their story as he did. He said they need someone honest and passionate. They must visit people that have never been subjected to the fundamentals of finance.

Someone must tell them not to take free credit cards and spend them. To help these people to perceive all the hidden evils and all the basic stuff that they need to know and have never learned (Grobar, 2020).

Or else those who have made it to stardom should raise their hands and declare it was their responsibility and it's their fault that the people are suffering and no one has improved yet. Kevin also said we should want people to improve and become better than we are. He said he wants others to beat the best attempts he has made in life. There is currently a significant wealth gap between generations.

Kevin Hart said, "It's your kids, it's your friends...you are supposed to live a certain way, do certain things to setup for the next generation to come and be able to do better" (Famousquotes123, 2022); (World Commission on Environment and Development, 1987).

How to Create Financial Freedom

Here are a few ways you could build generational wealth.

Invest

To recap on prior investment information: Long-term wealth building is achieved through the stock market. It is a fantastic alternative if you want to start creating generational wealth, as it can expand as the years go by.

Low-cost index funds will be the best place to start, as they maintain a low fee and expand over the long run. Another significant long-term wealth accumulator is real estate. It has the potential to bring in consistent cash flows. It brings long-term value growth, making it a dependable way to accumulate wealth and security.

Build a Business

Family-owned enterprises have less than a 30% chance of being passed down to the next generation (Tharawat Magazine, n.d.).

It's rare for family businesses to carry on into the next generation, but it's feasible that yours will. There is a chance that your kids choose to run the business you established if your interests and skills match theirs. Or even sell it for a profit.

It would help if you involved your children in the workings of the business from an early age, as I am sure you want to increase the likelihood of a successful transition. They should ultimately understand how the company runs and carry the same passion as you so they can succeed in the work you have established.

Invest in Your Kids' Education

Education frequently paves the pathway for your kids to sustain themselves in life. Many people with college degrees often seek well-paying careers that can get them on the right path with their finances.

Anyone with a degree will continue to have it, although other aspects of their life can change. Nobody can rob you of your education. If you can assist your children in graduating from college debt-free, you will be preparing them for a better financial future compared to many of their contemporaries.

Federal debt from student loans typically totals $37,787. The amount might increase even further in the future. Investing in their education is a fantastic strategy to build generational wealth and prepare your kids for financial success! Below are a few ways to begin saving for it (Haughn, 2023):

- Open an equity loan

- Consider opening an Education Savings Account

- Activate a 529 plan

- Purchase mutual funds

- Consider investing in a qualified savings bond

- Fund a custodial account with money

Teach Children About Personal Finance

Knowledge is the most powerful tool you can provide your kids with. There are various ways to chat about money with your children. For instance, children can learn about finances through activities, this book, or simply by listening to you discuss financial matters.

Describe the distinction between wants versus necessities. Show them how your retirement amount has increased over the years. As a result, it's vital to instill the idea that money shouldn't just be used for purchases, but it can be used to save.

You could show children how to be frugal when doing grocery shopping and how you would pay for the items and show them the receipt and what you saved. Saving money is not merely a wise financial practice.

No, it teaches patience and delayed gratification on how to set goals in making plans. Saving can also emphasize being ready to take on other responsibilities as it boosts morale and encourages security.

Give your children a piggy bank or savings container and encourage them to put coins in it. Other money that can be saved is their birthday or holiday money so that they can develop a habit of saving. To emphasize the value of saving money for the future, you, as a parent, can also assist your kids in opening their own bank accounts.

Write a Will

Anyone can create a will—you don't need an estate plan to have a will. It carries your precise instructions for when you can no longer speak. It's a detailed plan that shows your assets and what you have accumulated.

Without a will, relations between surviving family members can become tense. Emotions run high when a close family member passes, so when precise instructions are given in a will, ugly situations can be avoided, and financial hardship can be averted.

You can create your own will online; however, you must ensure it conforms to all requirements to be recognized as a legitimate will. In addition, your bank will execute an estate plan as trustee and executor; the staff can assist in informing you and your immediate family regarding the trust.

Name Your Beneficiaries

Even if you have a small inheritance, it's still vital to designate your beneficiaries—the person/s or organizations receiving your estate after you pass away. If you don't designate your beneficiaries, your assets, or a portion of them, may go to people or charities you didn't choose.

If you fail to identify beneficiaries correctly or write them down wrong, this could lead to complications. Ensuring that the correct procedures are followed, and the names and id numbers are written down correctly is essential.

Prompt

- Think about one person you plan to speak to in connection with creating a new habit you are starting. Then call them up right now!

- Describe the habit and explain how it will help to change your life for the better.

    o State if it will be a minor or significant change in how it impacts your life.

Chapter 7

Own Your Own House

"For women, financial independence is a matter of necessity" by Carrie Schwab-Pomerantz.

Being able to support yourself financially without outside help is financial independence. Everyone should strive to be economically secure, but this has been incredibly challenging for women as we have been under-represented throughout history and still struggle to gain equality in the workplace.

Looking at the 1700s and the 20th century, one of the most protracted and significant conflicts included the right for a woman to own property. Until women could legally own property, assets left to them in a will or any other inheritance had to be controlled by their husbands or another male family member.

The absence of legal protection was noteworthy, as it constrained a woman's financial independence. Among the most significant pieces of property legislation passed in American history was the Married Women's Property Act of 1848.

It served as a model for the rest of the legislation to follow, allowing single women further down the line the right to own and manage their own property. Right now, women in the United States are fully permitted to own their own property.

Although single women buy less than 20% of properties each year, today, women own more homes than single men (Winke, 2023). Stories of strong-willed women are emerging now, and this gives other women the encouragement needed to take full advantage of our rights, as Danielle did in this next story.

After graduating college, Danielle Desir Corbett lived with her mother, hoping to purchase her own home one day. She claimed that she had made a conscious effort to pay off her school loan debt and save as much money as possible.

Danielle was able to finish paying off $63,000 in debt from student loans using money she earned from her previous full-time employment and numerous side jobs that she took on. Once she had paid off all her debt, she would have enough money saved up for a seamless transition when purchasing her house (Huggins, 2022).

Daniele also mentioned that she frequently faced resistance from her family, who didn't think she should buy a home as a single woman.

While it is true that there has been inconsistent progress toward gender equality, those who contend that women are assuming leadership roles in the workplace can be shown how mistaken they are by examining employment pay equity and political participation statistics.

Women currently fill half of the jobs that men previously held. Many women working in sweatshops or factories have much more freedom and choices now.

Gender analysis is often done to examine the participation of men and women in paid labor working conditions. However, women placed in areas of influence frequently experience a daily onslaught of sexist behavior from men, even though this is prohibited in the workplace throughout many nations.

Women have been under-represented within management roles, and some groups have a more significant gender wage gap, according to data figures published by the Census Bureau (2021).

Approximately 44% of the workforce is female, but only 41% have been given managerial roles. In general, women make around $0.82 to the dollar a man makes. Yet there are cases where Latin or Hispanic women have made around $0.58 to the dollar, while black women have made around $0.63 for every dollar a male earns.

With respect to education, there were also differences in the gender pay gap. Women with bachelor's degrees had the smallest gap compared to men in a similar situation. In contrast, those that didn't quite have a high school diploma or its equivalent had the most significant paying gap compared to the men in the same situation.

We may observe how multiple communities deal with numerous interrelated problems at once when we view the world through an intersectional feminist lens. Building a society that excludes no one requires solidarity, challenging the power systems, and expressing views against inequality.

If you are a woman with a single, divorced, married, or widowed status, it should never determine your way of living. Never let anyone take away who you are and dictate how you should live out your life.

In an interview with *Time*, American professor of law Kimberlé Crenshaw, who once used the phrase intersectional feminism in 1989, described it as a prism for recognizing how many types of oppression typically interplay and exacerbate each other.

That involves expressing who you really are and not being ashamed to be a woman without worrying about criticism or jokes that are lashed out. Being successful is living the life you desire, but not only in a materialistic sense. It's about living your life to the fullest and pursuing your goals without waiting on others to fulfill your needs.

She claims that not all inequity is produced equally. An intersectional perspective demonstrates how people's social identities can overlap, resulting in compounded discrimination.

Kimberlé Crenshaw said, "We frequently discuss racial inequality in isolation from inequalities related to gender, class, sexual orientation, or immigration status. The fact that some people are affected by all of these things and the experience as a whole is frequently overlooked" (Steinmetz, 2020).

A woman should earn equal to a man for their work. How can that be argued? If they both do the same amount of work, they should be paid the same amount.

Money will decide the house you buy, the car you drive around, what food you eat, and what opportunities there are to sculpt your life. When you can own your money, you are entitled to make the decisions, but when you let someone else take control of your money, they can use it against you.

Many of the privileges that women take for granted were fought for and achieved during the 1900s by women activists and campaigners. It's simple to overlook how recently the struggle took place.

Megan Markle reminds us of how recently, when speaking to a group of women at the world conference, she claimed that she is a feminist. She said she seemed to stumble into it 20 years ago at the age of 11. Her class was listening to a program, and a commercial about Proctor and Gamble dishwashing liquid came on.

The commercial claimed, "That women all over America are fighting greasy pots and pans." Two boys behind Megan Markle said, "Yeah, that's where girls belong, in the kitchen."

She recalled feeling angry and hurt that she was seen as inferior. She asked her dad what he thought, and he encouraged her to write letters. Her 11-year-old mind decided to cover all her bases, and she began to write a letter to First Lady Hillary Clinton.

Then she wrote to Linda Allerbee and Gloria Allred and informed them of her findings. After that, she wrote a letter to Proctor and Gamble. In no time, Megan received letters back from all 3 of the ladies.

Not long after that, a camera crew arrived at Megan

Markle's house with First Lady Hillary Clinton. A month later, listening to the commercial, it said, "People from all over America are fighting greasy pots and pans." She immediately realized the magnitude of her actions.

She went on to say that it's not enough to talk about indifferences, and it's not enough to believe. Women must become more active and work on this problem. Statistics show that women's rights have only grown by eleven percent in twenty years.

Megan Markle said, "studies show that at the current rate, the elimination of gender inequality won't be possible until 2095" (Markle, 2018).

Further action will pave the way for quicker progress in a gender-equal and sustainable future. Gender inequality also includes income and finances. You can take an informative stand and be part of a change when you educate yourself.

———

Five Tips for Being Financially Free No Matter What Your Relationship Status Is

Are you in charge of the family finances? Do you know how much your household pays for each bill? Do you understand the different tax benefits when you file your taxes each year?

If you answered no to all or some of those questions, you are not alone. However, it's not too late. Imagine living a life that puts you in charge of your money rather than having it manage you or be managed by someone else. Good money management leads to financial freedom; it takes effort, sacrifice, and time, but still, the effort is worthwhile.

Are you prepared to discover how to create a financially secure future for your family and yourself? Below are five tips to help you get started.

Tip 1: Learn About Personal Finance

Spend time learning more about your finances; this includes your income, your partner's income, and your expenditures. Do they align with your values and personal goals? Are you aware of your spending patterns?

By understanding your finance, you can work on plans for the future, setting out goals, and building your credit. When you make the effort, you will keep control, and your money will stay secure, and your bills will be paid.

So that you stay in the habit, set a reminder on your phone or use the app for your banking to check in regularly.

Tip 2: Negotiate, Negotiate, Negotiate

The gender pay gap is real; generally, there is a $0.15 to $0.22 gap for every dollar in private and government organizations. To ensure the salary package is flexible, it's also a great idea to investigate the position and the company before taking the role (U.S. government accountability, 2022).

There are some work positions where the compensation rate is predetermined. That ensures that gender won't be a factor in the compensation conversation. Still, it only sometimes means fair pay across the market. So be sure to check market rates for similar positions.

When you approach the compensation conversation in your hiring process or even later when you're advocating for more pay, be sure you aren't starting on the wrong foot. Dr. Jonah Berger, a professor in marketing at The Wharton School and the author of *The Catalyst*, stated that 98% of the time, we start by driving at demands expecting it will eventually work in our favor and we will get what we want.

Berger instructs us to first approach with a highlight on our similarities. For instance, have a conversation and express your excitement over the offer and your desire to work with the individual by saying, "It's wonderful to be in a situation where we share the same goals, since I know you have seen dozens of candidates before deciding on me."

As a result, you are no longer on an antagonistic footing, and the recruiting manager is free to speak more candidly and see you as a member of the same team. Finding out what matters to the candidate is the next stage," according to Berger.

"The recruiting manager has a stake in the discussion as well. Ask yourself, what do they need to accomplish right now? Perhaps it is to close a vital skill shortage. It may be to show firm leadership and they are looking for specialized technical expertise, or perhaps it's addressing key skills in a strained marketing team. So how would you achieve your goals with that knowledge? If you know where another prospective employer can give you flexibility and where they can't," Berger explained, "you can conveniently suggest a compromise (Dr. Jonah Berger, 2013).

This includes making a trade-off on travel opportunities, a gym/fitness membership, or flexible working hours. For instance, if working hours mean a lot to you throughout the week, you can ask for flexibility to work a few hours on the weekend.

So, request whatever you want. After that, pay close attention to what the hiring manager says. If you are silenced, respond unaggressively, such as, "Wow, that's interesting. Could you elaborate on the reasoning behind that?"

"By posing the appropriate inquiry, you can begin to

direct the conversation, comprehend constraints, and perhaps create leverage or reach a compromise. In some ways, the fact that you are promised a set amount, can be a drawback because you may not have the opportunity to negotiate. When you do have the option to negotiate, do so and consider every angle" (Dr. Jonah Berger, 2013).

Consider the offer closely, and relate it to your current position. Then consider your future employment opportunities and the positions you have applied for. Before negotiating, consider the extras, such as stock options, retirement plans, and other bonus perks. Below are a few benefits you can negotiate on:

- alternative start dates

- additional 401(k) contributions

- extra paid time off or vacation

- flexible work schedules or remote work

- a transfer option to a different branch or office

- a recruitment bonus (can be linked to a relocation stipend)

- a remuneration bonus further on during the year

- percentages in equity or stock options

- set-up fees for home offices

- reimbursements for telephone, internet, or co-working space

- opportunities for outside training or professional growth

- help to cover a percentage of childcare or if there is a nearby daycare

- a budget for direct reports

- an improved job title that will boost your resume

- compensation for travel costs such as fuel, accommodation, and food

Understand which employee benefits are frequently negotiable. Keep in mind that if you accept this position, your future wages are based on the bargaining you have set up. Carefully evaluate whether you should counter an offer or if it's a reasonable offer before accepting. Below are jobs that frequently have a fixed-salary level:

- low-level positions in hospitality, retail, and customer service

- hourly paid roles

- an apprentice or beginner position and jobs in unions

- civil service

- other careers in government

Tip 3: Make and Save Your Own Money

Beyond a traditional income from a job, you can work towards making additional money by setting up a side business. As a stay-at-home mother, you don't need to feel left out. There are ways to generate passive money. Below are a few ideas you can ponder over:

- consult – offer your expertise at a price to other businesses.

- launch a print-on-demand enterprise

- attempt affiliate marketing

- influencer marketing – find a niche and create content for them

- babysitting

- become an online tutor

- promote an online course

- sell or rent out items you no longer need

Save for Emergencies

Always, always, always save for a rainy day, so you never feel anything but in control. You can still contribute to the house and still save a portion. You should set up an emergency fund in an account that offers flexibility without imposing restrictions—a high-interest nest egg or investments in the money market. Ally, Barclays, Citizen, and Citi all offer online savings accounts with above 3.5% annual percentage yields.

Tip 4: Before Having a Baby, Run the Numbers

Practice living on a lower income if you don't have access to paid leave or you are planning to take more unpaid time. This will assist you in identifying extra costs that you can cut back on or do without. Below are a few situations that need to be taken care of:

- Verify you have the necessary benefits, which include short-term disability.

- Ask if your workplace will offer paid leave.

- Determine the number of weeks covered and the proportion of your used salary.

- Find out if you have to use your sick and vacation days first. If so, save them up!

- Be aware of exactly how and when your benefits will be paid out, mainly if multiple sources are involved. You don't want to email your benefits provider one week after giving birth to determine the specifics regarding your leave payments.

USDA Reports on the Cost of Having a Child

Since 1960, the USDA has tracked the expenditure of raising a child. According to the most recent Consumer Expenditures Survey statistics, a household with parents that are married with 2 children in a middle-income range from $59,200 to $107,400 will spend about $12,980 per child, per year, in 2015 Lino, 2020. The estimated cost per child is anywhere from $18,000 to $19,000 and counting (Bhattarai et al., 2022).

This amount includes food, housing, and other requirements. When raising a child to the age of 17, middle-class, married parents can anticipate spending $233,610 (approximately $284,570 when expected inflation prices are taken into account). The price of a college education is not included in this amount.

What happens to the money? With a 29% share of all child-rearing expenses in middle-class families, living costs are the highest single expense. Food comes in second at 18%, followed by daycare at 16% for those who can afford it. These prices are according to the child's age, costs, and living area.

Additionally, costs rise as your child gets older. When we look at the cost from the infant to toddler duration, annual expenses were, on average, roughly $300 lower than that of teenagers between the ages of 15 and 17, as they average $900 and higher (Khazan, 2020).

Teenagers eat more food, and their clothing and transportation tend to grow along with them. This is also the age when they start driving; thus, the insurance cost increases or a second car is bought for them.

Additionally, regional diversity was noted. The most significant bill was spent on children by families in the Northeast urban area, followed by those in the West urban areas, South urban, and Midwest urban. The least amount of costs were spent on children in rural areas averaging about 27%.

Childcare and Schooling Costs

The cost of raising children is susceptible to the efficiencies of scale. That is, costs for each child decrease when there are more children, compared to families with 2 children. Expenses for married couples with 1 child worked out to be more on average.

The average cost per kid in households with 3 or more

children was 24% lower than the cost per child in a family with 2 children. The "cheaper by the dozen" factor is another name for this phenomenon (Lino et al., 2017).

Extra children cost less because families often buy food in larger quantities, making it more economical; children share bedrooms, pass down clothing and toys, and frequently babysit younger siblings.

The University of Michigan's Research

Research from the University of Michigan examined the lives of 657,061 American women who gave birth between 2008 and 2015 and received health insurance via their employers.

The most current year that the statistics were accessible was 2015, and all expenses were then adjusted for inflation. All the insurance costs and claims that are not covered regarding procedures and treatments the mothers used were tallied up within the year leading up to and during the three months following the delivery.

According to the study, mothers had to pay an average of $4,314 for vaginal deliveries in 2015, an increase of $2,910 from 2008. In contrast, the out-of-pocket expense for a cesarean delivery increased from $3,364 to $5,161. The average price for all deliveries indicated in 2015 was $4,500.

Michelle Moniz, an obstetrician-gynecologist at the University of Michigan's Von Voigtlander Women's Hospital as well as the study's primary author, adds, "I don't have many patients that have that amount of cash just hanging around. I occasionally witness people who are unable to pay for their medical care making decisions to forgo care altogether" (Khazan, 2020).

The techniques or technology used in birthing hasn't become that much more expensive over time. The increased deductibles and copays, lump amounts that insurance companies need their clients to pay first before they contribute any money, are the main culprit, according to the study's authors.

In fact, as businesses look to push medical costs onto employees, numerous Americans over recent years have been caught with all these high deductibles. In the latest study, Moniz and her coworkers discovered that, over a 7-year span, the proportion of women having deductibles increased from roughly 69% to almost 87%.

As a result, women became responsible for paying a more significant portion—about 7% more on their delivery costs (Khazan, 2020). Reading studies can be an excellent beginning point for gathering and understanding existing techniques as well as reducing lessons to enhance woman-centered quality care regardless of the socioeconomic status of women.

If the SDG era's stated goal is to "leave no one behind," indeed. In that case, the investigation should be made into the excessive, pointless, or prohibited expenses used when women access maternal health treatments.

There is no doubt about it, raising children is rewarding, but the cost can get overwhelming. However, if you plan accordingly, having children can be beautiful and not cause you and/or your partner financial stress.

Tip 5: Build Your Credit

If you obtain a credit card and adopt the philosophy of "just spending what you have," it can help you to get a mortgage or a car loan when you previously couldn't. Consider the nine strategies below when building your credit:

1. Strategically pay off credit card balances.

2. Request increased credit limits.

3. Become a registered user.

4. Pay debts promptly.

5. Challenge mistakes made in credit reports.

6. Handle accounts for collections.

7. Apply for a secured credit card.

8. Obtain credit from utilities and rent payments.

9. Expand your credit portfolio.

Take the money you saved and use it on whatever you choose. Pay for a hiking tour, or soccer camp or get your hair done. You can make a difference by taking an informative stand and educating yourself. Look at the following women's stories to see how they've managed their money.

Everyday Woman

Usually, women don't boast about their wealth, but in this chapter, they do, so other women and their daughters can learn a lot from them. Below are stories of everyday women who took the initiative to invest, and it paid off.

Emma Gordon

Life continued as usual while we were undergoing a divorce; we had bills to pay, gadgets that needed fixing, and house repairs and maintenance all around. I was experiencing financial difficulty since I was left with no other means of support than my wage to hold my house together.

I began using You Need a Budget (YNAB) (an app that creates a budget) on my daughter's advice, who is in college. I ran out of money during the second weekend of my first month; this filled me with fear. I only receive payroll once a month, so my initial month using YNAB was disastrous.

Nevertheless, I racked up a massive record of victories a year after I began. At month's end, there was still money remaining. I started to pay my credit card off. I used the funds I had on hand to cover the $1,800 cost of car maintenance.

Whenever a life event occurs, such as a marriage, divorce, baby, death, change in employment, or loss of jobs, you can either feel frustrated, helpless, and overwhelmed, or you can think about the situations you can control.

I chose to concentrate on my finances. I listen to friends and family and invest in deals where it's a win-win situation. I have done well at times, and it has boosted me. Certain days are more complex than others, but that's life. In addition to what I anticipated, having financial control has made me feel a lot happier.

Ellen Roseman

Ellen Roseman is a Toronto-based consumer advocate, author, and personal finance expert. "In the first decade of the 1990s, I began trading with a broker. Later, at the beginning of 2008, I launched an investment club.

I am writing to express my gratitude to a woman who spoke to our group in 2011 about Constellation Software, a global supplier of industry-leading services and software to various businesses in both the private and the public sectors.

She informed us that now would be an excellent time to buy because the OMERS (retirement fund) was about to sell its holding in the company at $110 per share. I purchased a little position, but over time it just kept expanding. I have already sold half of my stock at least twice, and it's been a massive success.

The firm is trading at roughly $1,200, about 20% below its previous highs. Constellation only provides a modest dividend. Generally, I prefer purchasing equities that offer dividends. I made an exception since the CEO possesses a special knack for identifying profitable businesses to buy. I am so happy it worked for me" (Steward, 2021).

Rachel Dugmor

Living paycheck to paycheck, Rachel's family of seven had what seemed like a string of constant emergencies. Their car brakes gave out one month, their heater needed to be replaced the next month, and their roof started leaking the following month. They constantly ran out of money due to unforeseen costs. Each month, they had to sit down and prioritize which emergency needed to be resolved first and how much they needed to put aside to keep food on the table.

Every budgeting strategy imaginable had been tried, but her income fluctuated wildly from month to month, and nothing ever worked out. She stumbled upon an app, You Need a Budget, in 2015 and immediately became enamored.

Rachel said that YNAB functions similarly to the envelope system, except the situation was virtual. Those earlier crises became less of an issue as we learned to live on last month's money. I maintained my credit cards, as they stayed paid off, and I started making payments towards my debt.

When bills were due, they got paid. We weren't constantly struggling for money; the never-ending financial fight ended. As a family, we advanced over the years and are doing well now. We have two homes, three cars, and almost impeccable credit. Budgets with anticipated incomes and expenses are always set up for four to five months.

We have jumped to being entirely free of heavy credit card debt from being completely swamped in debt and living from paycheck to paycheck. I never imagined that we would have an expanding savings account. The payments were all paid for, an emergency buffer has been put in place, and extra funds are now available.

When the extra funds reach a certain amount, I invest the money. I have also had one or two failed attempts when investing, but I didn't lose a lot. It's hard for me to envision not working on a budget since it has been a key to my success.

Elizabeth Holmenlund, CFA, VP at Morgan Stanley

I wasn't sure what I intended to pursue in life. I was awarded a few scholarships and awards from various foundations in Denmark in addition to the great government education assistance from the Danish state.

All these factors held me in good stead to go to the U.K. and attend an economics school in London. Although I knew nothing about investment banking, I began my employment and education at the LSE, and I developed a passion for the financial industry.

I worked at J.P. Morgan in London after graduating, where I spent nearly six years. Finally, at this point, I felt able to oversee and invest my money. I decided to keep my interests in J.P. Morgan to a minimum since I was conscious of the importance of diversification, given that the business posed the most significant risk to my employment.

I acquired stock options (assuming a position in which you will profit if the price of the pound declines) as part of my benefits package. Many employees kept their stock as they progressively matured over time. I planned to constantly sell my stock as it matured to diversify any risk.

This method is not exclusive to J.P. Morgan, though owning it may have been a wise investment. For me, it was purely a risk-management tactic and highly profitable. I also found that converting the whole of my pound sterling bonuses into dollars was amazingly effective.

I know it's nearly impossible to outperform the market, but I don't believe my intelligence puts me above the competition. Why try, then? Additionally, I work all day looking at investments. **Hence,** I also don't want to do it in my spare time! I only invested in the MSCI World ETF, which had a return of +30% in 2016—my most extraordinary year ever" (Steward, 2021).

Prompt

- Write down one tip that resonated most with you from the 5 above.

- Write down how you will begin to implement that tip into your everyday life.

  - Take a few minutes now to execute on that tip, whether it's doing research on your market rate or learning more about one new passive income stream.

Conclusion

"My father used to say that it's never too late to do anything you wanted to do. And he said, "you never know what you can accomplish until you try," by Michael Jordan

You are not alone in your financial struggle (Hardy, 2022). Americans collectively have had more financial difficulty since the pandemic started.

According to data released in February 2023 by the Census Bureau, more than 91 million Americans find it "somewhat difficult" or "extremely difficult" to afford everyday household expenses.

In the study conducted by the bureau between June 29, 2022, and July 22, 2022, 40% of Americans who responded fell into these two categories, and most acknowledged it to be "extremely difficult."

We have been railroaded into this problem due to a lack

of education and guidance, yet we can't dwell on this fact. We must move on to a brighter, more positive, and secure future.

Consider how different people's financial issues would be if everyone had an emergency plan, for starters, and their finances were in order before COVID-19.

Having an emergency reserve is typically regarded as just a short-term financial objective. In a mechanical sense, that is accurate. However, establishing an emergency fund is among the wisest financial goals you could aim to achieve because it has significant long-term advantages.

Let's go over just a few of the advantages of possessing an emergency plan that is adequately stocked:

- It alleviates a lot of your financial stress or worries as you will always have a reserve in case you find yourself in a bind.

- It's in line with what it's intended for—an emergency fund will be available to soften the impact in the case of an emergency like a job loss or a considerable medical expense.

- It's an essential tool for managing your money. If you can save money for an emergency fund, then you can save money for whatever other financial goals you may have.

- It gives you access to an intermediary financing source that serves as a kind of bridge between your salary/wage and your investment accounts. This helps you to avoid interfering with your protracted investments.

- Simply maintaining an emergency fund can help you cope with the emotional ups and downs of the stock market since you won't be in danger if it crashes.

When you consider all the advantages of having a robust emergency fund, it should bump its importance up the list of priorities a few notches.

Now, having a budget promotes financial stability. A budget also simplifies saving money for significant purchases like a car or home by keeping track of costs and sticking to a plan.

It enables you to pay bills on time and accumulate funds to invest. Overall, having a budget gives a person more monetary sustainability for both their short- and long-term standing.

Investing is a successful approach to using your money and increasing your fortune. Your cash may see value growth that exceeds inflation if you make wise investment decisions. The potential of compound interest and the trade-off between risk and return is the leading causes of higher growth prospects.

Year after year, costs of living increase and debts mount, and you rarely catch up if you don't invest. As individuals, we need to delve into opportunities and create a financial net for ourselves to live the life we desire.

Keep asking yourself, what do I want from life? What do I hope to achieve in my lifetime? Your list of goals should be kept close to where you can refer to them since reaching your goals is a long-term endeavor that requires constant motivation.

Make sure you have everything you need to keep yourself motivated, whether it's scheduling a bimonthly dinner with friends, paying for a streaming service, or going to a concert. You won't stay driven if you don't allow yourself to have a little fun.

Please do it for your family, but most of all, do it for yourself because you deserve it. Don't let this book be another situation you forget and settle with the norm, adopt the "just do it" attitude.

Don't land yourself in debt if you haven't already. Regardless of your situation, you can change it. Just stay focused and disciplined on your goals. You need to prioritize your retirement funds by starting to save now for your retirement.

Make sure that when setting up your retirement plan, you will have enough money to maintain a reasonable level of living if you stop working full-time or cut back on your hours. Take advantage of the 401(k) fund if you have one at your current workplace, which allows you to save money for retirement. Or open your own Solo 401K or Roth IRA with trusted companies like Vanguard.

Please share your story with your friends and family, then listen and learn from them about their successes or failures in life. This will put you in a good position for the future. Recall what good advice you learned from successful people mentioned in this book.

The first step in learning how to handle your money is to gain knowledge through experience. You can learn how to manage your wealth effectively and efficiently by observing those who are financially successful and have conquered their financial mountain. This is referred to as "standing on the shoulders of giants." Honestly, why should we reinvent the wheel?

All said and done! Let's encapsulate those 15 tips below that we learned as we worked through the book.

1. Understand what you need financially to achieve your goal.

2. Pick a realistic budgeting framework.

3. Commit to your budget.

4. If you get a promotion or increase in your income, don't inflate your lifestyle—add that additional money into savings.

5. Find an alternative utility and insurance provider—you can't imagine the savings you could find.

6. Pay more on your debts, mortgages, and loans every month, if you can.

7. Setup an emergency fund.

8. Get debt free.

9. Avoid loans where possible but understand that they are sometimes a necessary evil.

10. Invest.

11. Prepare for retirement.

12. Build multiple sources of income.

13. End the taboo.

14. Stay financially free.

15. Create generational wealth.

Being broke in certain respects can be a blessing as it allows you to learn financial lessons that would otherwise be incomprehensible. The intent of this book and my goal is not to promote "being broke," but rather to emphasize the advantages of experiencing it.

People who have experienced poverty or hit rock bottom are typically the most equipped to cope with unanticipated losses in the future, if they are willing to learn from the past.

Now that you possess all the resources use them! Don't fear the unexpected because now you are prepared to handle it. Make mistakes, as they result from future successes, not failures.

What will you accomplish when you change your financial mindset?

Leave a Review

As an independent author with a small marketing budget, reviews are my livelihood on this platform. If you enjoyed this book, I'd really appreciate it if you left your honest feedback and tell me one financial goal you are determined to achieve. You can do so by submitting a review on the platform where you purchased *Personal Finance for Young Adults*.

References

Amazons Watch Magazine. (2022, June 21). *For women, financial independence is a matter of necessity.* Amazons Watch Magazine. https://www.amazonswatchmagazine.com/on-the-marble/for-women-financial-independence-is-a-matter-of-necessity/

Ayoola, E. (2023, January 4). *Self-employed retirement plans: Know your options.* NerdWallet. https://www.nerdwallet.com/article/investing/retirement-plans-self-employed#TraditionalRoth

Bayte-White, C. (2023, January 24). *Calculate penalties on a "401 k" early withdrawal.* Investopedia. https://www.investopedia.com/articles/personal-finance/082515/how-do-you-calculate-penalties-401k-early-withdrawal.asp

Bhattarai, A., Keating, D., & Hays, S. (2022, October 13). *What does it cost to raise a child?* Washington Post. https://www.washingtonpost.com/business/interactive/2022/cost-raising-child-calculator/

BrainyQuote. (2022). *Johann wolfgang von Goethe quotes*. BrainyQuote. https://www.brainyquote.com/quotes/johann_wolfgang_von_goeth_104453

Burke, M. (2016, October 4). *6 immigrant stories that will make you believe in the american dream again*. Forbes. https://www.forbes.com/sites/monteburke/2016/10/04/6-immigrant-stories-that-will-make-you-believe-in-the-american-dream-again/?sh=162693b08027

Center on Budget and Policy Priorities. (2021, September 10). *Tracking the covid-19 economy's effects on food, housing, and employment hardships*. Center on Budget and Policy Priorities. https://www.cbpp.org/research/poverty-and-inequality/tracking-the-covid-19-economys-effects-on-food-housing-and

Daily Burst Of Energy. (2020, October 8). *Discipline is everything – best self discipline motivational speech*. Daily Burst of Energy. https://dailyburstofenergy.com/discipline-is-everything-best-self-discipline-motivational-speech/

Davel, R. (2020, July 17). *Breaking the poverty mindset in africa*. WORK 4 a LIVING. https://work4aliving.org/a-grandmothers-legacy-breaking-the-yoke-of-poverty-thinking-in-bizana-south-africa/

Dr. Jonah Berger. (2013, March 13). *Contagious: Jonah Berger on why things catch on.* Knowledge@Wharton. https://knowledge.wharton.upenn.edu/article/contagious-jonah-berger-on-why-things-catch-on/

Dunn, E., & Courtney, C. (2020, September 14). *Does more money really make us more happy?* Harvard Business Review. https://hbr.org/2020/09/does-more-money-really-makes-us-more-happy

Elkins, K. (2019, July 11). *Shaq: As soon as I started investing like Jeff Bezos, I probably quadrupled what I'm worth'.* CNBC. https://www.cnbc.com/2019/07/11/shaquille-oneal-says-he-invests-like-jeff-bezos.html

Famous Quotes 123. (2022). *Kevin Hart quotes on people, love, work and time.* Famousquotes123. https://www.famousquotes123.com/kevin-hart-7572.html

Fay, B. (2021, May 13). *The U.S. consumer debt crisis.* Debt. https://www.debt.org/faqs/americans-in-debt/

Foster, S. (2022, February 8). *Combating the racial wealth gap: 9 money moves for individuals of color.* Bankrate. https://www.bankrate.com/banking/savings/closing-the-racial-wealth-gap/

Get early bird, S. (2022, April 15). *Everything you need to know about generational wealth.* Get Early Bird.

https://www.getearlybird.io/blog/generational-wealth#:~:text=Simply%20put%2C%20generational%20wealth%20is

Goodreads, S. (2023, January 31). *Karon Waddell quotes.* Goodreads. https://www.goodreads.com/author/quotes/15107446.Karon_Waddell

Gracious Quotes, S. (2020, December 2). *107 Robert kiyosaki quotes (rich dad poor dad).* Gracious Quotes. https://graciousquotes.com/robert-kiyosaki/

Grobar, M. (2020, August 18). *Kevin Hart cancels culture's' bad environment' and defends Ellen & Nick cannon: "I know who they are."* Deadline. https://deadline.com/2020/08/kevin-hart-dont-fk-this-up-emmys-netflix-controversy-interview-news-1203015498/

Hardy, A. (2022, July 22). *40% of Americans are struggling to pay their bills right now.* Money. https://money.com/difficulty-paying-bills-census/

Haughn, R. (2023, February 7). *Student loan debt statistics in 2022.* Bankrate. https://www.bankrate.com/loans/student-loans/student-loan-debt-statistics/#:~:text=Key%20student%20loan%20debt%20statistics

Hernandez- Kent, A., & R.Ricketts, L. (2021, January 5). *Wealth gaps between white, black and hispanic families in 2019| st. Louis fed.* Stlouisfed. https://www.stlouisfed.org/on-the-economy/2021/january/wealth-gaps-white-black-hispanic-families-2019

Hernbroth, M. (2019, July 13). *Shaquille O'Neal says he quadrupled his net worth after adopting an investment strategy he learned from Jeff bezos.* Business Insider. https://www.businessinsider.co.za/shaq-net-worth-jeff-bezos-investment-strategy-2019-7

Huggins, T. (2022, August 9). *5 women on how they bought a home on their own.* The Balance. https://www.thebalancemoney.com/5-women-on-how-they-bought-a-home-on-their-own-6385755

Khazan, O. (2020, January 6). *The high cost of having a baby in america.* The Atlantic. https://www.theatlantic.com/health/archive/2020/01/how-much-does-it-cost-have-baby-us/604519/

Lino, M. (2020, February 18). *The cost of raising a child.* Usda. https://www.usda.gov/media/blog/2017/01/13/cost-raising-child

Malhotra, D. (2017, December 5). *15 rules for negotiating a job offer.* Harvard Business Review.

https://hbr.org/2014/04/15-rules-for-negotiating-a-job-offer

Manton, E. J., English, D. E., Avard, S., & Walker, J. (2006). *What college freshmen admit to not knowing about personal finance.* Journal of College Teaching & Learning (TLC), 3(1). https://doi.org/10.19030/tlc.v3i1.1758

Mint. (2023, February 13). *Elon musk valuable advice shared by billionaire: 'Don't attach yourself...'* Mint. https://www.livemint.com/news/world/elon-musk-valuable-advice-shared-by-billionaire-don-t-attach-yourself-harsh-goenka-11661140702271.html

Mr Great Motivation, S. (2022). *Milton hershey.* Mr Great Motivation. https://www.mrgreatmotivation.com/2018/10/milton-hershey.html

O'Shea, A. (2021, March 12). *How to invest in real estate: 5 ways to get started.* NerdWallet. https://www.nerdwallet.com/article/investing/5-ways-to-invest-in-real-estate

Passiton. (2017). *"There is no exercise better for the heart than reaching down and lifting people up."* Passiton. https://www.passiton.com/inspirational-quotes/7235-there-is-no-exercise-better-for-the-heart-than

Patel, D. (2019, April 22). *Richard Branson's 8 keys to*

happiness and success. Entrepreneur.
https://www.entrepreneur.com/living/richard-bransons-8-
keys-to-happiness-and-success/331932#:~:text=Don

Quora, S. (2014). *The illiterate of the 21st century will not be those who cannot read and write but those who cannot learn, unlearn and relearn. Alvin Toffler. do you agree or disagree?* Quora. https://www.quora.com/The-illiterate-of-the-21st-century-will-not-be-those-who-cannot-read-and-write-but-those-who-cannot-learn-unlearn-and-relearn-Alvin-Toffler-Do-you-agree-or-disagree

Quotefancy. (2022). *Alan Kay quote: 'The only way you can predict the future is to build it.'* Quotefancy.
https://quotefancy.com/quote/1266487/Alan-Kay-The-only-way-you-can-predict-the-future-is-to-build-it

Quotefancy. (2023, February 14). *Maya angelou quote: 'Hoping for the best, prepared for the worst, and unsurprised by anything in between.'* Quotefancy.
https://quotefancy.com/quote/4908/Maya-Angelou-Hoping-for-the-best-prepared-for-the-worst-and-unsurprised-by-anything-in#:~:text=Maya%20Angelou%20Quote%3A%20%E2%80%9CHoping%20for

Ramsey Solutions. (2022, November 10). *What is passive income, and - how do I build it?* Ramsey Solutions.

https://www.ramseysolutions.com/retirement/what-is-passive-income

ResumeBuilder. (2023, January 19). *Job market difficulties continue in 2022, as employers fail to meet job-seekers' expectations.* ResumeBuilder. https://www.resumebuilder.com/job-market-difficulties-continue-in-2022-as-employers-fail-to-meet-job-seekers-expectations/

Sarah. (2023, February 7). *How to build generational wealth.* Clever Girl Finance. https://www.clevergirlfinance.com/blog/generational-wealth/

Smith, M. (2020, October 14). *HelpGuide.org.* HelpGuide. https://www.helpguide.org/articles/mental-health/cultivating-happiness.htm

Steinmetz, K. (2020, February 20). *She coined the term "intersectionality" over 30 years ago. Here's what it means to her today.* Time. https://time.com/5786710/kimberle-crenshaw-intersectionality/

Steward, B. (2021, March 8). *Five investing success stories from five international women.* CFA Institute Enterprising Investor. https://blogs.cfainstitute.org/investor/2021/03/08/five-investing-success-stories-from-five-international-women/

Tharawat Magazine, S. (n.d.). *What is the economic impact of family businesses?* Tharawat Magazine. https://www.tharawat-magazine.com/economic-impact-family-businesses/

Thomas Edison. (2022). *Edison quotes.* Thomas Edison. https://www.thomasedison.org/edison-quotes#:~:text=%E2%80%9COpportunity%20is%20missed%20by%20most

Thomson, J. (2022, August 18). *Talking about money is taboo. You should break it.* Big Think. https://bigthink.com/sponsored/money-discussions-taboo/#:~:text=What%2C%20then%2C%20is%20the%20reason

U. S. Government Accountability. (2022, December 15). *Women in the workforce: The gender pay gap is greater for certain racial and ethnic groups and varies by education level.* GAO Government Accountability. https://www.gao.gov/products/gao-23-106041#:~:text=In%20private%2C%20for%2Dprofit%20companies

Vega, N. (2021, July 15). *Nearly 40% of couples who live together don't know how much their partner makes—experts say that's a problem.* CNBC. https://www.cnbc.com/2021/07/15/40-percent-of-couples-who-live-together-dont-know-how-much-partner-makes.html

Whiteside, E. (2022, September 17). *What is the 50/20/30 budget rule?* Investopedia. https://www.investopedia.com/ask/answers/022916/what-502030-budget-rule.asp

Wiener-Bronner, D. (2018, April 26). *How Richard Branson went from high-school dropout to billionaire entrepreneur.* CNNMoney. https://money.cnn.com/2018/04/26/news/companies/richard-branson-rebound/index.html#:~:text=He%20was%2015%20when%20he

Winke, R. (2023, January 27). *History of women's property rights and ownership.* Family Handyman. https://www.familyhandyman.com/article/women-property-rights-history/

World Commission on Environment and Development. (1987). Report of the world commission on environment and development: Our common future towards sustainable development 2. Part II. common challenges population and human resources 4 (p. 16). *United Nations.* https://sustainabledevelopment.un.org/content/documents/5987our-common-future.pdf

Wrightone, S. (2019, April 8). *'The only person who never makes a mistake is the person who never does anything" ~ Theodore Roosevelt.* Wrightone. https://wrightoneconsulting.com/the-only-person-who-never-makes-a-mistake-is-the-person-who-never-does-anything-theodore-roosevelt/#:~:text=~THEODORE%20ROOSEVELT-

Yaged, C. (2016, August 5). *How Nicolas Cage wildly spent a $150 million fortune.* FinanceBuzz. https://financebuzz.com/finance-nicolas-cage-buying-spree

Yochim, D., Coombes, & Ayoola, E. (2023, January 6). *Best retirement plans: Choose the right account for you.* NerdWallet. https://www.nerdwallet.com/article/investing/best-retirement-plans-for-you

Youtube. (n.d.). *15 minutes of Kevin Hart dad jokes | Netflix is a joke.* Youtube. https://www.youtube.com/watch?v=gbxSpLDQehg

Made in the USA
Las Vegas, NV
06 January 2024

83996414R00098